DATE DUE

INTIMATE
VIOLENCE
IN
FAMILIES

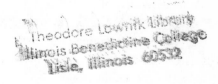

FAMILY STUDIES TEXT SERIES

Series Editor: RICHARD J. GELLES, *University of Rhode Island*
Series Associate Editor: ALEXA A. ALBERT, *University of Rhode Island*

This series of textbooks is designed to examine topics relevant to a broad view of family studies. The series is aimed primarily at undergraduate students of family sociology and family relations, among others. Individual volumes will be useful to students in psychology, home economics, counseling, human services, social work and other related fields. Core texts in the series cover such subjects as theory and conceptual design, research methods, family history, cross-cultural perspectives, and life course analysis. Other texts will cover traditional topics, such as dating and mate selection, parenthood, divorce and remarriage, and family power. Topics that have been receiving more recent public attention will also be dealt with, including family violence, later life families, and fatherhood.

Because of their wide range and coverage, Family Studies Texts can be used singly or collectively to supplement a standard text or to replace one. These books will be of interest to both students and professionals in a variety of disciplines.

Volumes in this series:

1. LATER LIFE FAMILIES
   Timothy H. Brubaker

2. INTIMATE VIOLENCE IN FAMILIES
   Richard J. Gelles & Claire Pedrick Cornell

Volumes planned for this series:

THEORIES OF FAMILY LIFE, David M. Klein

THE PATHS OF MARRIAGE, Bernard Murstein

FAMILY RESEARCH METHODS, Brent C. Miller

WORK AND FAMILY LIFE, Patricia Voydanoff

FAMILY POWER, Maximiliane Szinovacz

BECOMING A PARENT, Ralph LaRossa

FAMILY STRESS, Pauline Boss

DIVORCE, Sharon J. Price & Patrick McHenry

REMARRIAGE, Marilyn Ihinger-Tallman & Kay Pasley

CONCEPTUAL FRAMEWORKS FOR FAMILY STUDIES,
   Keith Farrington

INTIMATE VIOLENCE IN FAMILIES

Richard J. Gelles
and
Claire Pedrick Cornell

FAMILY STUDIES TEXT SERIES 2

SAGE PUBLICATIONS
Beverly Hills London New Delhi

For information address:

SAGE Publications, Inc.
275 South Beverly Drive
Beverly Hills, California 90212

SAGE Publications India Pvt. Ltd.
C-236 Defence Colony
New Delhi 110 024, India

SAGE Publications Ltd
28 Banner Street
London EC1Y 8QE, England

Printed in the United States of America

Library of Congress Cataloging in Publication Data

Gelles, Richard J.
  Intimate violence in families

  (Family studies text series ; v. 2)
  Bibliography: p.
  Includes index.
  1. Family violence—United States. I. Cornell,
Claire Pedrick II. Title. III. Series.
HQ809.3.U5G443   1984   362.8′2   84-18066
ISBN 0-8039-2232-9
ISBN 0-8039-2233-7 (pbk.)

FIRST PRINTING

To the Memory of Barry A. Marks

Contents

Acknowledgments

THIS BOOK OWES MUCH to our previous work and writings on family violence. A number of our colleagues and friends have been particularly helpful over the years and assisted in considering the difficult and complex issues that surround family violence. Murray Straus has been a teacher, colleague, and sounding board for the past twelve years. Eli and Carolyn Newberger and the entire Family Development Study at Children's Hospital Medical Center, Boston, have also been colleagues and friends for over a decade. They opened up the world of clinical practice to us, and their help and support have been invaluable. Bud Bolton also helped guide us through the trials and tribulations of applying research to practice and policy. Finally, our students at the University of Rhode Island, especially the students in Sociology 313X: Family Violence, have provided us insight and useful ideas for a text on family violence.

Betty Jones has typed our manuscripts for eleven years. We are sure that her spelling was much better before we totally confused her with our own creative attempts.

Finally, our respective spouses, Winton Cornell and Judy Gelles, provided critical social and emotional support. Jason Gelles (aged 10) and David Gelles (aged 7) were also sources of motivation—often, their first words after getting off the school bus were: "How many pages did you write today?"

CHAPTER

1

Introduction

PEOPLE ARE MORE LIKELY to be killed, physically assaulted, hit, beat up, slapped, or spanked in their own homes by other family members than anywhere else, or by anyone else, in our society. Some observers (Straus, Gelles, and Steinmetz, 1976) have proposed that violence in the family is more common than love.

Not only are these facts true today, but they are true throughout the history of the United States. Not only do these statements apply to American families, but they are also accurate assessments of family life in England, Western Europe, and many other countries and societies around the globe.

We do not commonly think of the family as society's most violent social institution. Typically, family life is thought to be warm, intimate, stress reducing, and the place that people *flee to* for safety. Our desire to idealize family life is partly responsible for a tendency to either not see family violence or to condone it as being a necessary and important part of raising children, relating to spouses, and conducting other family transactions.

This text is designed to provide a basic overview of the subject of family violence. Many books take a look at only one aspect of violence and maltreatment in the home. Typically, a writer will discuss child abuse, wife abuse, or elderly abuse; but very rarely do books and articles attempt to examine all aspects of violence in families and try to look at the whole picture of family violence. While it is important to understand the nature and causes of child abuse or wife abuse, concentrating on just one form of violence or abuse may obscure the entire picture and hinder a complete understanding of the causes and consequences of abuse. A case example of the problems produced by narrowly focusing on just one type of abuse is illustrated by the experience of a hospital-based child abuse diagnostic team. The team was discussing the case of a six-month-old child who had received a fractured skull. After reviewing the medical reports and results of interviews with both parents, it was concluded that a five-year-old sibling had caused the damage by striking the infant. All in the room breathed a sigh of relief. Now, they concluded, they would not have to file a child abuse report. Just as they were about to break up, satisfied with the consensus they had arrived at, a physician commented, "But how do you suppose the five year old learned to be violent?" Back they went to the table for a two-hour discussion about whether or not the violence of a five year old was cause for a child abuse report.

This case illustrates dramatically that one form of family violence may be closely connected to other acts of violence in the home. To focus on just one type of family violence often causes one to miss the overall picture. As important, especially for this text, is that one can only understand, explain, treat, and prevent family violence by understanding the operation and function of the entire family system.

MYTHS THAT HINDER UNDERSTANDING OF FAMILY VIOLENCE

How is it possible that families have been violent for centuries, all over the globe, and only recently have we discoverd and attended to family violence as a serious family and social problem? How is it that after twenty years of intensive research and practice in this field, we can still read newspaper accounts that talk about instances where children who were identified by social service agencies as abused, and whose cases have been followed by social workers for months, are killed, virtually under the nose of the person who was supposed to protect them? One answer for these two questions is that there are a number of myths about family violence that tend to hinder both public recognition of the problem and effective professional practice. This text is designed to explode many of the conventional myths about family violence and replace these myths with knowledge derived from scholarly research on family violence. As a preview of the issues that will be taken up in the text, and as a means of clearing the decks of some of the more popular and persistent myths, this section presents and then debunks the major myths hindering our understanding of family violence.

Myth 1: Family Violence Is Rare

Until the 1960s, most people considered family violence a rare phenomenon. What few official statistics there were tended to bear out this assumption. Few states required professionals or members of the public to report known or suspected instances of child abuse. When David Gil surveyed the entire country in 1967 to determine how many valid cases of child abuse there were, he found that there were about 6000 (1970). The numbers of abused children varied state by state, speaking more about the procedures used to locate abused children than the actual occurrence of abuse. California had more than 3500 reports, Rhode Island none. There were, and still are, no agencies that gather data on wife abuse, parent abuse, or sibling abuse. Prior to 1970, few hospitals bothered to categorize women patients they treated as either abused or nonabused. Police departments did keep records of how many domestic disturbance calls they received and investigated, but many times the records were inaccurate or incomplete. Sometimes a husband who assaulted his wife would be recorded as a domestic disturbance, other times it would be recorded as an assault.

The strong belief that families are places people turn *to* for help, and the perception that city streets hold the greatest risk for women and children, help to continue the myth of the rareness of family violence even into the 1980s. As different types of family violence are discovered and examined, most people find it difficult to believe how many individuals and families are involved in violence in the home.

Myth 2: Family Violence Is Confined to Mentally Disturbed or Sick People

A woman drowns her twin six-month-old daughters. Another mother throws her daughter off a bridge into icy water. A mother and father plunge their four year old into a bathtub filled with boiling water. A father has sexual intercourse with his six-month-old daughter. A woman waits for her husband to take a shower, then fires a bullet into his skull at close range with a .357 magnum.

These descriptions, and accompanying color slides of the harm done to the victims, are usually enough to convince most people that only someone who is mentally disturbed or truly psychotic would inflict such grievous harm onto a defenseless child, woman, or man. One way of upholding the image of the nurturant and safe family is to combine the myth that family violence is rare with the myth that only "sick" people abuse family members. Combining the two myths allows us to believe that when and if violence does take place, it is the problem of "people other than us." An example of this is the manner in which family violence is portrayed in literature, television, or the movies. The sociologists Murray Straus and Suzanne Steinmetz (Steinmetz and Straus, 1974) reviewed American fiction, television shows, and movies for examples of family violence. First, they found violence between family members infrequently portrayed. When there was an incident of violence, it almost always involved a violent act committed by someone who was a criminal (the violent son in the movie *The Godfather*), foreign (the comic strip "Andy Capp"), or drunk (Rhett Butler in *Gone With the Wind*). The message conveyed by the media is that normal people do not hit family members.

The manner by which people determine that abusers are sick undermines the claim of mental illness. "People who abuse women and children are sick," we are told. How do you know they are sick? "Because they abuse women and children." This explanation does nothing more than substitute the word "sick" for "abuse." The key question is, without knowing what someone did to his or her spouse or child, could you accurately diagnose him or her as mentally ill? In most cases, this is impossible. The sociologist Murray Straus (1980) claims that fewer than 10 percent of all instances of family violence are caused by mental illness or psychiatric disorders.

Myth 3: Family Violence Is Confined to the Lower Class

Next to the myth of mental illness, the next most pervasive myth about family violence is that it is confined to the lower class.

Like all myths, there is a grain of truth behind this belief. Researchers do find more reported violence and abuse among the lower class. The psychologist George Levinger studied applicants for divorce and learned that 40 percent of the working-class applicants indicated that abuse was the reason they were seeking the divorce. Of the middle class applicants 23 percent also mentioned violence as the motivation for wanting to end the marriage (Levinger, 1966). Official reports of child abuse indicate an overwhelming overrepresentation of lower class families being reported as abusers. However, by virtue of being in the lower class, families run a greater risk of being correctly *and falsely* labeled "abusers" if their children are seen with injuries (Newberger et al., 1977). Believing that abuse of wives and children is confined to the lower class is yet another way people try to see acts of others as deviant and their own behavior as normal.

Myth 4: Family Violence Occurs in All Groups— Social Factors Are Not Relevant

When the first medical practitioners began to notice and attend to cases of child abuse, one of the first things they were struck by was that the children came from every type of social, racial, economic, and age group. This finding shattered the myth of violence being confined to the lower class, but that myth was replaced by the belief that social factors were not related to child abuse and family violence. If the children of lawyers, doctors, and corporate executives are being abused along with children of unemployed truck drivers, how then could social class or poverty be a cause of child abuse?

There are two problems with this observation and the belief that social factors are not relevant in explaining family violence. First, for a factor to be a cause of child abuse does not mean that it has to be perfectly associated with abuse. For poverty to be a causal factor, it is not necessary that only poor people abuse children and no well-to-do people are abusive. There are very few (perhaps no) perfect associations in social science. Thus, for social factors to be causal, they need only satisfy the four criteria of causality: (1) association (statistical, not deterministic); (2) time order (the cause must precede the consequences); (3) the relationship is not spurious (no third factor, preceding cause and effect in time, is related to both cause and effect); and (4) rationale (the proposed relationship has to make logical sense). The second problem with the observation that social factors are not related, is that they are. Even though abuse can be found among the wealthy and the poor, it is more likely to be found among the poor. Even though most poor people do not abuse their children, there is indeed a greater risk of abuse among those in the lowest income groups. We will examine the relationship between social factors and family violence in Chapters 3 and 4.

Myth 5: Children Who Are Abused Will Grow Up to Be Child Abusers

This is a myth with some truth value to it. Virtually all studies of child abuse find that abusive adults were more likely to have been treated harshly and abused as children than adults who are not abusive. The problem with the statement that "Children who are abused will grow up to be child abusers," is that this is a deterministic statement and the relationship is probabilistic. People who experience abuse are *more likely*, but not pre-programmed to become violent adults. Sadly, many people have begun to believe that *all* abused children grow up to be violent. This belief has two sad and negative consequences. First, it scares people who have experienced violence as children into thinking that they are "preprogrammed" to be violent and that perhaps they should avoid marriage and having children. Second, those who are responsible for detecting and treating child abuse may see an unusual injury in a child and, upon learning that a parent had been battered as a child, assume that the parent has caused the injury. False positive diagnoses (labeling someone an abuser when they are not) are a possible consequence of believing that violence determines violence.

Again, just as with social factors, it is important to remember that perfect associations rarely exist in social science. Abuse and violence grow out of a complex set of interrelated factors (as we will find in Chapters 3 through 5), and latching onto one common sense factor misrepresents the causal explanation and can cause injustice.

Myth 6: Battered Wives Like Being Hit, Otherwise They Would Leave

Once, after viewing David Susskind interview six battered women, a well educated, intelligent man commented, "What I don't understand is what the wives did to cause their husbands to hit them, and if they really didn't like getting hit, why didn't they (the wives) just pack up and leave?" Battered women fail to attract the same attention and sympathy directed toward battered children because somehow, many people think that the women (a) provoked the violence and (b) must like it if they didn't leave after the first beating. Those who espouse this view (and it is a belief of both men and women) tend to be those with considerable education, good jobs, and extensive social networks. They cannot imagine that someone could be socially, legally, and materially entrapped in a marriage. They cannot imagine that a woman could literally have no place to go. Wives seem to bear the brunt of considerable "victim blaming." Quite a few people believe that battered wives are somehow culpable, and their culpability is enforced by their decision not to leave. Nothing could be further from the truth. This issue will be discussed at length in Chapter 4.

Myth 7: Alcohol and Drug Abuse Are the Real Causes of Violence in the Home

The "demon rum" explanation for abuse in the home is nearly as popular as the mental illness explanation, and perhaps more popular than the two social class myths. Again, certain facts help support the myth. Most studies find a considerable association between drinking and violence (Gillen, 1946; Guttmacher, 1960; Wolfgang, 1958; Gelles, 1974; Snell, Rosenwald, and Robey, 1964). In cases of spousal violence, both offender *and* victim have frequently been drinking before the violence. Perhaps as many as half the instances of violence and abuse involve some alcohol or drugs—a very strong association. But, do the drugs or the alcohol themselves cause people to be violent? Are drugs, and is alcohol, a disinhibitor which unleashes violent behavior? And, would solving the drug or drinking problem eliminate the

violence? Common sense frequently says "yes" to these questions. Research argues "no." There is little evidence that alcohol
and drugs are disinhibitors. The best evidence against the
disinhibitor theory comes from cross-cultural studies of drinking
behavior. These studies find that how people react to drinking
varies from culture to culture (MacAndrew and Edgerton, 1969).
In some cultures people drink and become violent, in others,
people drink and are passive. What explains the difference? The
difference is due to what people in those societies believe about
alcohol. If they believe it is a disinhibitor, people become
disinhibited. If they believe that it is a depressant, people become
depressed. Because our society believes that alcohol and drugs
release violent tendencies, people are given a "time out" from the
normal rules of social behavior when they drink or when people
believe they are drunk. Combine the time out with the desire to
"hush up" instances of family violence, and you have the perfect
excuse: "I didn't know what I was doing, I was drunk." Or, from
the victim's perspective, "My husband is a Dr. Jekyll and Mr.
Hyde—when he drinks he is violent, when he is sober there is no
problem." In the end, violent spouses and parents learn that if
they want to not be held responsible for their violence, they
should either drink before they hit, or at least say they were
drunk.

Myth 8: Violence and Love
Do Not Coexist in Families

Once people believe that families are violent, they tend to think
that the violence occurs all the time. Moreover, the persistent
belief is that if family members are violent, they must not love one
another. Violence, while common in many families, is certainly
not the most frequent behavior in the home. As we will see in
Chapters 3, 4, and 5, although violence and abuse are typically
chronic problems in families and not simply one-shot events, on
average, abusive parents and partners are violent about once
every other month. The remaining time the family functions
nonviolently (although the threat of physical violence and abuse
tends to hang heavy in the air). It is not only possible, but
probable that abused wives still have strong feelings for their

husbands. Many battered children love their parents in spite of the beatings. In fact, most victims of family violence are taught that they deserve the beatings, and thus they have the problem, not the attacker. That violence and love can coexist in a household is perhaps the most insidious aspect of family violence, because we grow up learning that it is acceptable to hit the people you love.

WHAT IS VIOLENT AND ABUSIVE?

One of the earliest and most enduring problems in the field of child abuse, wife abuse, and family violence has been to develop a useful, clear, and acceptable definition of "violence" and "abuse." Those who have studied child abuse have tried for years to develop an acceptable and accepted definition, and have found that after countless conferences, workshops, and publications there are perhaps as many definitions as there are scholars in the field.

An example of an early definition of child abuse was the one used by C. Henry Kempe and his colleagues (1962) in their article "The Battered Child Syndrome." Kempe, a physician, defined child abuse as a clinical condition (i.e., with diagnosable medical and physical symptoms) having to do with those who have been deliberately injured by a physical assault. This definition restricts abuse to only those acts of physical violence which produce a diagnosable injury. The National Center on Child Abuse and Neglect, an agency of the Federal Government established in 1974, expanded the definition of abuse to include nonphysical acts as well. The agency's definition of abuse is

the physical or mental injury, sexual abuse, negligent treatment, or maltreatment of a child under the age of eighteen by a person who is responsible for the child's welfare under circumstances which indicate that the child's health or welfare is harmed or threatened thereby [Public Law (93-237)].

This definition lumps acts of violence and nonviolence into the same definition. On the one hand, definitions like those used by the National Center on Child Abuse and Neglect include acts that go well beyond physical violence. On the other hand, this definition is restrictive in that *only* acts of violence that cause an injury are considered abusive.

Force and Violence

If a father takes a gun and shoots at his child and misses, there is no physical injury, and according to many definitions of abuse, this act is not abuse. There is, of course, harm in a father shooting and missing, but the act itself does not qualify as abuse under the strict terms of the definitions. Ideally, then, a definition of abuse should include harmful acts that, for some reason (bad aim) do not produce an injury. At the other extreme, a father who spanks his child is not usually considered either abusive or violent. Most people believe that spanking a child is normal, necessary, and good. Nearly 90 percent of parents report that they spank their children, and some people believe that the true figure is a lot closer to 100 percent. As many as one in four men and one in six women think that under certain conditions it is appropriate for a husband to hit his wife (Stark and McEvoy, 1970). Consequently, some researchers believe that, in defining violence, it is a good idea to separate the so-called normal acts of "force" from the nonnormal and harmful acts of "violence." While such a separation might seem desirable, distinguishing between acceptable and unacceptable acts proves more difficult than one can imagine. One major question is: Who decides which acts of violence are legitimate and illegitimate? Is "force" hitting a child without physical evidence of an injury, while "violence" is hitting a child and causing a black and blue mark? Should the decision be left to the person who is being hit, to the person doing the hitting, to agents of social control such as police, social workers, or judges? Should the decision be left to social scientists? An extensive study of the definitions of child abuse carried out by Jeanne Giovannoni and Rosina Becerra found that what is defined as "child abuse" varies by social category and profession. Police officers, social workers, physicians, and lawyers have differing views on what constitutes "child abuse." Similarly, the definition of abuse varies by social class, race, and ethnicity (Giovannoni and Becerra, 1979).

A Definition of Violence

In the end, the difficulty in defining what acts are violent and what acts are physical, but not violent, is due to varying cultural and subcultural views on whether certain behavior is or is not acceptable. It would be far too complex to have a definition that depended on the situation the behavior was used in, the size of the offender, the size of the victim, and the reactions of those who observed or heard about the behavior. For that reason, this text uses the definition of violence employed by a number of researchers. The definition views violence as "An act carried out with the intention or perceived intention of causing physical pain or injury to another person." The physical pain can range from slight pain, as in a slap, to murder. In order to deal with the common sense assumption that spankings should be viewed differently from using weapons against wives or children, it is useful to consider two categories of the general definition of violence, "normal violence" and "abusive violence."

Normal violence. Normal violence is the commonplace slaps, pushes, shoves, and spankings that frequently are considered a normal or acceptable part of raising children or interacting with a spouse. These are the acts many people object to calling "violent." This is especially true of spanking. Family violence researchers who state their views on television or radio, or who are quoted in the press, constantly receive indignant letters from people who object to calling a spanking "violent." "Spare the rod and spoil the child." "I was spanked and I needed it." "My little one would be dead by now if I hadn't spanked him and let him know he shouldn't drink or eat certain things." These and other arguments, typically advanced by those who do the hitting, all focus on the physical acts that we consider "normal violence."

Abusive violence. The more dangerous acts of violence we shall refer to as "abusive violence." These acts are defined as acts that have the high potential for injuring the person being hit. Included in this definition are punches, kicks, bites, chokings, beatings, shootings, stabbings, or attempted shootings or stabbings.

The controversy in this definition is that it does not take into consideration what actually happened to the victims of the violence. By ignoring consequences, this definition is much broader than the more narrow definitions of child or wife abuse, which typically require that some diagnosable harm be inflicted. The reason for not being concerned about consequences is that research on assault and homicide, which has been carried out by criminologists, has consistently found that the things which differentiate injurious violence from violence that causes no harm are typically random phenomena such as aim or luck (Pittman and Handy, 1964; Pokorny, 1965; Wolfgang, 1958).

Why Just Physical Violence?

Hitting, punching, and shooting and other acts of physical violence do not exhaust the range of harmful acts committed by family members against other household members. Students of child maltreatment have identified neglect, emotional abuse, sexual abuse, educational neglect, medical neglect, and failure to thrive as forms of maltreatment. Feminists sometimes argue that pornography and some types of advertising are acts of violence against women (London, 1978). Why then, confine this book to only physical violence? One reason is because it is important, theoretically and practically, to differentiate acts of physical violence from other harmful but nonviolent coercive acts (Etzioni, 1971). Physical violence is qualitatively different from other means of injuring people. Thus, although physical violence shares with other harm-producing acts the central characteristics of malevolence and harm-doing intent, the nature of the intended harm—physical pain and suffering—is unique. As the childrens' taunt goes: "Sticks and stones may break my bones, but names will never hurt me." Well, the names sometimes do hurt, but in a very different way. From a practical point of view, lumping all forms of malevolence and harm-doing together may muddy the water so much that it might be impossible to determine what causes abuse. While harmful acts may share some causes, other factors may be (and are) unique. Unless violence is treated separately from other acts, it may be difficult to determine both the causes and solutions to family violence.

DISCUSSION QUESTIONS

1. Why is it useful to examine all forms of family violence instead of concentrating on just one single type, such as child abuse?

2. Why do the myths about family violence exist? What possible functions might the myths serve for people who treat family violence? For society?

3. Discuss and critique the "alcohol as a disinhibitor" theory of the relationship between alcohol and family violence.

4. Develop and critique your own definition of "violence" and "abuse."

SUGGESTED ASSIGNMENTS

1. Locate newspaper articles that report family violence. What definition of violence and abuse seem to be used in these articles? Are any of the myths included in the articles? Identify the common assumptions about the nature and causes of family violence in the articles.

2. Locate articles on child abuse, sexual abuse, or spouse abuse in popular magazines (e.g. *Women's Day*, *Redbook*, *Family Circle*, *Time*, *Newsweek*). Compare how this issue is presented to the presentation found in newspapers. Locate one or more of the myths presented in the chapter in the magazine articles.

CHAPTER
2

Violence Between Intimates

Historical Legacy—
Contemporary Approval

We encounter two different types of family violence nearly every day. The first, which produces the greatest outrage and the saddest emotions, are the newspaper and television reports of child abuse or wife abuse. These reports typically describe a case of a mother, father, or boyfriend who kills a defenseless infant or youngster, or the shooting deaths of a husband or wife at the hand of a partner. Although these reports are heard and read almost daily, they seem to be exceptions to normal family relations. The violence and abuse are so outrageous, so apparently senseless, that it does not seem possible that they could be committed by normal people in normal families. Reactions to such violence are typically swift and punitive. Mothers and fathers who kill their children are subjected to swift arrest and prosecution, and the public clamors for stern and severe punishment—ranging from imprisonment to sterilization. One legislator in Rhode Island, reacting to a particularly sensational case of child abuse, introduced legislation calling for the public hanging of parents who slay their children. Reactions to cases of a spouse killing a partner are typically less vehement and the calls for punishment more subdued; nevertheless, spousal violence still evokes pity for the victim and calls for "something to be done."

The second form of family violence is actually more common, less recognized, and rarely accompanied by public outrage and calls for punishment or sanction. A mother spanks her child in the supermarket. A husband grabs his wife's arm and pulls her away from someone at a cocktail party. Brothers and sisters who squabble and throw objects at one another are so common that they are nearly invisible. Unless the child who is hit in the supermarket suffers a bloody nose or an injury; unless the wife who is pushed, pulled, or slapped in public is hit with a closed fist; or, unless the siblings who fight cause a major physical injury, few people are deeply troubled by these events. Fewer people intervene or try to help the victim, and even fewer see these actions as similar in kind and consequence to the newspaper and television descriptions of child or wife abuse. Even with the daily newspaper accounts of family violence, most people cling to the myths that family violence is rare and confined to the mentally ill or psychiatrically impaired. Violence, however, is *not rare*, it is *not new*, and it is *not confined* to families in the United States. This chapter begins by examining the historical record on family violence and then considers the cross-cultural evidence. The historical and cross-cultural patterns are revealing because they provide a basis for understanding today's level of approval for intimate and private violence. It is our society's willingness to approve and accept many forms of violence in the home that is a central factor in explaining both individual instances of violence and the broader pattern of violence in families.

CENTURIES OF VIOLENCE AND ABUSE

Infanticide and the Abuse of Children

Today we take for granted that children have the right to live. In fact, the debate over abortion involves considerable discussion over whether this right should be extended to a fetus at the moment of conception. But, the right to live has not always been extended to newborns or infants. According to Samuel Radbill (1980: 3), in ancient times infants had no rights until the right to live was ritually bestowed. Parents had the ultimate authority to recognize children and their right to live. Typically, this right was invested primarily in the father. Without a "right to live," and dependent on a father's recognition and bestowing of the right, infants in ancient times could be slain. Indeed, infanticide, or the willful killing of newborn children, was widely accepted and widely practiced among ancient and prehistoric people. Infants could be put to death because they cried too much, because the family was already too large, because they were sickly or deformed, or because they had some perceived imperfection. Girls, twins, and children of unmarried women were especially vulnerable to infanticide (Robin, 1982).

Numerous rituals or survival tests were used to "test" the newborn. Radbill (1980: 4) notes that some North American Indians threw newborns into a pool of water and saved them only if they rose to the surface and cried. Exposing children to the natural elements was a classic test of survival, one used by the Greeks.

The Bible reminds us of other instances of infanticide or attempted infanticide. Genesis, the first book of the Bible, describes God's commandment to Abraham to sacrifice his son Issac. Later, Jesus was presumably saved from Herod's "slaughter of the innocents."

Infanticide was practiced through the Middle Ages, and, as Lloyd DeMause (1974) so graphically notes, by 1526 the latrines of Rome were said to "resound with cries of children who had been plunged into them." High rates of infanticide continued through the eighteenth and nineteenth centuries, especially among illegitimate children. Even today, an occasional case of an illegitimate child being slain surfaces. Recently, the newspapers and news weeklies reported the case of a trunk being discovered in Somersworth, New Hampshire. Inside the trunk were a number of small skeletons, alleged to have been illegitimate children killed at birth.

Violence and abuse of children was not limited to infanticide. From ancient times to colonial America, mutilation, violence, and abuse were not only condoned, but frequently mandated as appropriate ways of rearing children. Children were hit with rods, switches, and canes. Some were castrated to produce eunuchs. Puritan parents in colonial America were implored to "beat the devil" out of their children. Stubborn child laws, which allowed parents to put unruly children to death, hung over the heads of colonial children—although apparently these laws were rarely, if ever, invoked.

The historical record of the treatment of children is not entirely bleak. Children's rights were recognized, but slowly. The social historian Phillipe Aries (1962) notes that the concept of childhood did not appear until the Middle Ages. Before then, childhood ended almost when the child was weaned.

However, there is some evidence of child welfare and child protection as early as 6000 years ago. Children in Mesopotamia had a patron goddess to look after them; orphan homes existed in early Greece and Rome. Foster care is also mentioned in the historical discussions of child care.

Radbill (1980) reports that child protection laws were legislated as long ago as 450 B.C. when the father's complete authority over a child was modified. Numerous societies had rules and regulations concerning sexual relations and sexual access to children.

The case of Mary Ellen Wilson, an illegitimate child, is considered by most child welfare experts as a graphic illustration of the turning point in child welfare and concern for abused children. Mary Ellen was an illegitimate child, born in New York City in 1866 and a ward of the New York Department of Charities (Robin, 1982). A charity worker found eight-year-old Mary Ellen beaten and badly abused. Much to the charity worker's chagrin, neither the police nor the New York Department of Charities would provide aid for Mary Ellen. Mary Ellen's plight was brought to court, not by a human service agency, but by the Society for the Prevention of Cruelty to Animals.[1]

As a consequence of the Mary Ellen case, the Society for the Prevention of Cruelty to Children was formed. However, child protection efforts were hampered by unsophisticated diagnostic methods, limited availability of services, and lack of awareness of the problem in the larger society.

Medical technology advanced the diagnostic process and medical attention helped to advance advocacy on behalf of abused children. The pediatric radiologist John Caffey (1946) wrote on the use of X-ray technology to detect present and past inflicted injuries in children. In 1962, Henry Kempe and his colleagues published their seminal article "The Battered Child Syndrome" in the prestigious *Journal of the American Medical Association*. The Kempe article not only drew on Caffey's and others' work on X-ray diagnosis, but the article also implored physicians to diagnose this major pediatric problem.

Within a few years of the publication of the Kempe article, the federal government had drafted model child abuse reporting legislation. By the end of the 1960s all fifty states had passed reporting laws that mandated health care professionals to report suspected cases of abuse. In 1974, the federal government passed the Child Abuse Prevention Act, which among other things, established the National Center on Child Abuse and Neglect. The National Center was established to carry out research, to support and fund innovative prevention and treatment programs, and to serve as a national clearinghouse for information on the nature, causes, and means of treating and preventing child abuse and neglect.

While the funding for the National Center on Child Abuse and Neglect was modest (compared to other federal programs), the establishment of the center and the research and treatment programs it sponsored served to focus a national spotlight on the problem of violence and abuse of children.

Women: The Appropriate Victims

There were other victims of intimate violence in ancient times. Women not only failed to escape violence, they appear to be the preferred and most frequent victims of violence in the home. The sociologists Rebecca and Russell Dobash (1979: 32), claim that in order to understand wife beating in contemporary society, one must understand and recognize the legacy of women as the "appropriate victims" of family violence. Roman husbands and fathers not only had control over their children, but over their wives as well. Roman husbands had the legal right to chastise, divorce, or kill their wives. Not only that, but the behaviors for which these punishments were appropriate were the very same behaviors that Roman men engaged in almost daily—adultery, public drunkeness, and attending public games (Dobash and Dobash, 1979: 36-37).

Biblical accounts and descriptions of women further emphasize the appropriateness of blaming and punishing women for transgressions. Only Eve is blamed for eating the forbidden fruit in the Garden of Eden, and for this transgression, women are punished by having to bear children. The same passage in Genesis that multiplies women's sorrow and calls for them to bear children also provides for the husband to rule over women (Gen. 3:16).

The expression "rule of thumb" is said to come from old English common law, which stated that a husband could beat his wife with a rod no thicker than his thumb. With British law as a guide, colonists in America and their new government continued the tradition of permitting the chastisement of wives. Prior to the twentieth century, numerous states had laws that allowed hitting wives to enforce domestic discipline.

Some restrictions on the husband's behavior were legislated at the end of the nineteenth century. Alabama and Massachusetts passed laws in 1871 spelling out which actions were no longer permitted (Davidson, 1978). North Carolina repudiated the "rule of thumb" in 1874. Nevertheless, although limits were placed on husbands, they still had more leeway in acts of violence toward their wives than a stranger would have if he or she assaulted someone in a tavern.

There was no Mary Ellen for battered women. No technological breakthrough such as pediatric radiology to uncover years of broken jaws and broken bones. No medical champion galvanized the attention of the medical community. Instead, the discovery of the problem of battered women in contemporary society was a grassroots effort. Some social scientists had concerned themselves with violence toward women at the beginning of the 1970s, but attention to the problem came from women themselves. Erin Pizzey, a woman in the Chiswick section of London, set up a women's center for local women, and soon found her center filled with victims of battering. She produced a movie, "Scream Quietly or the Neighbors Will Hear," and a book (1974) by the same name, which captured attention in Europe and the United States. The National Organization for Women organized a task force to examine wife battering. Women's groups and feminist organizations organized safe houses, or shelters for battered women, roughly along the line of the Pizzey shelter in London. Still, in the 1980s wife battering has not received the same attention as has the abuse of children. While there have been some congressional hearings on wife abuse, there still (as of 1984) has been no national legislation similar to the Child Abuse Prevention Act. The Office of Domestic Violence, established in the late 1970s to operate along the lines as the National Center on Child Abuse and Neglect, was closed in 1981. More important, virtually no money was appropriated for research and treatment of the problem of wife abuse. If the existence of national programs and national legislation is a measure of social concern, then women are still considered more appropriate victims of family violence than children.

CROSS-CULTURAL PATTERNS OF VIOLENCE

As the previous discussion of the historical legacy of family violence illustrates, violence toward children, toward wives, and between family members is certainly not confined to the United States. It is very difficult, however, to compare precisely child abuse and wife abuse in the United States, or in other western countries, to family violence in other societies. The first problem is that present knowledge of child abuse and wife abuse is based almost entirely on research and clinical experience in western nations. According to Sheila Kamerman (1975) only the United States and Canada have specific legislation dealing with the reporting of child abuse. There is precious little firm data on the incidence of child abuse in countries other than the United States (and even in the United States, there seems to be an incidence statistic for every person who ever wrote on the subject of family violence). A third difficulty is that there is little consistency in the definitions of abuse and violence. The historical legacy of child and wife abuse has produced differing conceptions over what is, and is not, appropriate behavior in families. Thus, behavior viewed as abusive in one society could be considered normal in another society. These differing definitions make it quite difficult to compare research from various countries.

Despite the difficulties in defining violence and abuse cross-culturally, there are some tentative conclusions that can be drawn about the international nature of family violence.

Women Are the Most Likely Victims

The anthropologist David Levinson has examined the records of the Human Relations Area Files. These records contain descriptive and statistical information on a wide range of societies over time and around the world. Looking at sixty well-described small scale and folk societies, which represented all the major cultural regions of the world, Levinson (1981) found that wife beating was common or frequent in four out of ten societies. Physical punishment of children (there were no data on abuse) was common or frequent in one in four societies. Wife beating was rare in one in five societies, while physical punishment of children was rare in nearly four in ten societies (see Table 2.1).

Levinson's results show that there are many cultures in the world where caretakers rely on physical punishment of children far less often than in the United States (see the following chapter for a complete discussion on the extent of the use of violence towards children in the United States). Levinson's data also confirm the Dobashes' hypothesis that women are the preferred victims of family violence around the world.

Family Violence Is More Common in Developed Nations

Although definitions of violence and abuse vary from country to country, and although few countries have conducted scientific studies of the extent of either child or wife abuse, descriptive and clinical information indicate that child and spouse abuse are more common in Western, industrialized, developed nations such as the United States, Great Britain, Germany, and France. Developing nations also seem to have problems of abuse and violence, but these seem to be grounded in the social disorgani-

34   INTIMATE VIOLENCE IN FAMILIES

TABLE 2.1
Relationship Between Physical Punishment and Wife Beating

| | Physical Punishment | | | |
Wife Beating	Rare	Infrequent	Frequent	Common
Rare	Andamans Copper Eskimo Ifugao Iroquois Ona Thailand	Rural Irish Hopi Trobrianders		
Infrequent	Kanuri Lapps Lau Mataco Tucano	Klamath Masai Ojibwa Pymies Santal Taiwan Tikopia Tzeltal	Ashanti Cagaba Garo Pawanee Wolof	
Frequent	Bororo Iban Tarahumara	Kapauku Korea Kurd Toradja	Azande Dogon Somali	Amhara
Common	Chuckchee Tlingit Yanoama	Aymara Hausa	Ganda Truk	Serbs

SOURCE: Reprinted with permission from D. Levinson, "Physical Punishment of Children and Wifebeating in Cross-Cultural Perspective," in *Child Abuse and Neglect* 5 (4), Pergamon Press, Ltd. 1981.

zation caused by modernization and the resultant changes in family, clan, tribal, and social situations. The People's Republic of China is frequently described as a society with little or no problem with child or wife abuse, although Westerners familiar with patterns of child rearing in China forty or fifty years ago tend to doubt this assertion. Scandinavian countries are also described as having little or no problem with child or wife maltreatment. This is generally thought to be due to social conditions being good, the widespread use of contraceptives limiting the number of unwanted children, free abortions, and the fact that many mothers work and can leave their children with day-care institutions (Vesterdal, 1977). Levinson's review of child punishment and spouse abuse in sixty societies confirms the finding from anthropological fieldwork that hunting and gathering societies rarely treat children harshly (1981).

Cultural Attitudes Toward Women and Children

One conclusion of cross-cultural research on family violence is that researchers rarely find one central factor that explains abuse or violence in all societies. Korbin (1981), for instance, found that many present-day Chinese who were abused by their parents did not become abusing parents themselves in contemporary China. This is contrary to the consistent finding in the United States and other western countries that children who are abused run a higher risk of growing up to be abusive than children who are not abused. Many of the factors that predict abuse in one society will not be predictive in another (Edgerton, 1981). Nevertheless, some factors are important across societies. Korbin (1981: 208) briefly summarizes the factors related to child abuse as

1. cultural value of children,
2. beliefs about certain categories of children,
3. beliefs about age capabilities and developmental stages of children, and
4. embeddedness of childrearing in kin and community networks.

Briefly, if children are valued for economic, spiritual, or psychological qualities, they are less likely to be maltreated. If certain types of children have less desirable qualities, such as being illegitimate, orphans, stepchildren, females, retarded, or deformed, they are likely to be abused. Maltreatment often depends on what a society thinks children are capable of. Finally, if there is a network of concerned childrearers beyond the biological parents, this too reduces the risk of abuse. The Dobashes (1979) find similar trends in the cross-cultural record of wife beating. Wife beating depends to a great extent on cultural attitudes about women. The more women are viewed as the property of their mates, the greater the risk of their abuse. The more women are dependent on their mates, the more likely they are to be mistreated.

Finally, Levinson points out that the presence of punishment of children in societies is related to wife beating. If physical punishment is rarely used in a society, then wife beating is far more likely to be absent than present (Levinson, 1981).

CONTEMPORARY ATTITUDES

Violence between family members has a historical tradition that goes back centuries and cuts across continents. It should come as no surprise that contemporary social scientists have proposed that in the United States and many other countries, "the marriage license is a hitting license" (Straus et al., 1980). Numerous surveys and situations emphasize the point that today in the United States many people believe that, under certain circumstances, it is perfectly appropriate for a husband to hit his wife. The parents who fail to hit their children are considered to be deviant, not the parents who hit.

At the end of the 1960s the U.S. Commission on the Causes and Prevention of Violence carried out a study of violence in the United States. The primary reason for the study was to try and understand the causes of the tragic rash of assassinations and riots that plagued the country between 1963 and 1968. Along with the questions on public violence, the commission asked a number of questions about private violence. Among the conclusions was that about one-quarter of all adult men, and one in six adult women, said they could think of circumstances in which it would be all right for a husband to hit his wife or for the wife to hit her husband (Stark and McEvoy, 1970). The same survey found that 86 percent of those surveyed agreed that young people needed "strong" discipline. Of the sample, 70 percent thought that it was important for a boy to have a few fist fights while he was growing up.

Fifteen years after the U.S. Commission on the Causes and Prevention of Violence conducted their research, the sociologists Murray Straus, Richard Gelles, and Suzanne Steinmetz carried out the first national survey on family violence. Their questions of people's attitudes toward violence in the home confirmed the findings from earlier research. Just under one in four wives and one in three husbands thought that a couple slapping one another was at least somewhat necessary, normal, and good (Straus et al., 1980: 47). More than 70 percent of those questioned though that slapping a twelve-year-old child was either necessary, normal, or good.

Anecdotal accounts further underscore the widespread cultural approval of private violence. In 1964 a young woman named Kitty Genovese was returning home to her apartment in the Queens section of New York City. She was accosted and repeatedly stabbed by a man; and, while a number of her neighbors heard her screams for help and watched the assault from windows, no one called the police. The young woman's death led many people to conclude that American society was corrupt, since bystanders seemed too apathetic or unwilling to get involved in a homicide. However, upon closer examination, it was suggested that the apathy of Kitty Genovese's neighbors was not the result of their lack of concern, or the fact that they were immune to violence after years of watching television. Rather, many of the witnesses thought that they were seeing a man beating his wife, and that, after all, is a family matter.

In Worcester, Massachusetts, a district court judge still sits on the bench and tries an occasional wife abuse case despite the fact that he is a wife beater who misrepresented his behavior under oath during a divorce trial (D'Agostino, 1983).

Millions laughed (and still laugh) when Jackie Gleason would rant "Alice, you're going to the moon" while shaking an angry fist at his television wife in the popular program, *The Honeymooners.*

Fairy tales, folklore, and nursery rhymes are full of violence against children. Hansel and Gretel, before they were lured into the gingerbread house, had been abandoned by their parents to starve in the forest because money was scarce. Snow White was taken in the woods to be killed by the huntsman on the order of the wicked queen who was her stepmother. Mother Goose's "Old Woman Who Lived in a Shoe" beat her children soundly and sent them to bed. "Humpty Dumpty" is a thinly disguised metaphor for the fragility of children, and "Rock a Bye Baby," with the cradle falling from the tree, is not even thinly disguised.

SUMMING UP

The chapters that follow document the extent of intimate violence in the United States today, consider the factors that are associated with acts of family violence, examine the various theories which have been brought to bear to explain violence in the home, and finally consider methods of treating and preventing family violence. The tragic nature of family violence and the emotions that are stirred up as a result of specific instances of child, wife, or elder abuse, frequently focus our attention on the immediate situation or on a specific case. It is important to keep in mind that what we are experiencing is neither new nor particularly unique to our own society. While we look for causes and solutions in individuals, or families, or even in communities, we should remember that cultural attitudes about women, children, the elderly, and cultural attitudes about violence as a means of self-expression and solving problems are at the root of private violence. We will see that income, stress, and other social-psychological factors are related to acts and patterns of domestic violence, but we need to consider that people have choices as to how they will respond to stress, crisis, and unhappiness, and the historical and cultural legacy of violence in the home is a powerful means of influencing what choices people consider appropriate. Sociologists David Owens and Murray Straus (1975) found that experience with violence as a child is one of the most powerful contributors to attitudes that approve of interpersonal violence. We now turn to an examination of violence toward children.

DISCUSSION QUESTIONS

1. Why are women considered the "appropriate" victims of family violence?

2. Identify the problems which hamper our ability to compare the extent of family violence in other western and non western societies to the extent of family violence in the United States.

3. Using Jill Korbin's 5 factors that are related to a society's rate of child abuse, explain why the rate of child abuse in the United States is high compared to the rate of child abuse in Scandinavian countries.

SUGGESTED ASSIGNMENTS

1. Read the Old and New Testaments of the Bible and identify examples of family violence (implicit or explicit).

2. Read some Mother Goose nursery rhymes and identify themes or messages that seem to condone violence and abuse of children. Find other children's stories or fables that convey the same message.

3. Watch Saturday morning cartoon shows and count how many violent acts are included per ten-minute segment.

NOTE

1. Legend has it that the reason Mary Ellen's case was taken on by the Society for the Prevention of Cruelty to Animals was that Mary Ellen was designated an "animal." Apparently, the truth of the matter is that the charity worker who found Mary Ellen appealed to the founder of the society, who took the case on because of human concern, rather than as an official of the society (Robin, 1982: 17).

The Youngest Victims

Violence Toward Children

SUE WAS A SINGLE PARENT who lived in a fourth floor walk-up apartment. Her husband had left her three years earlier, and child support payments stopped within weeks of the final divorce decree. Poverty and illness were as much a part of Sue's home as the busy activity of her four-year-old daughter Nancy. One cold gray March afternoon, Sue took Nancy out for a walk. Together they hiked up the steep pedestrian walkway of a suspension bridge that rose up behind their apartment. At the top of the bridge, Sue hugged Nancy and then threw her off the bridge. Sue jumped a moment later.

Miraculously, both Nancy and Sue survived. Both were plucked from the icy water by a fishing boat. Nancy, with major internal injuries, was rushed to a nearby hospital, and Sue, remarkably without major injury, was sped to a different hospital. Nancy joined the thousands of children each year who are admitted to hospitals for child abuse. Her case, and that of her mother, was starkly clear. An intentional act designed to grossly injure, harm, or kill a child. The child abuse team at the hospital that admitted Nancy had little trouble diagnosing Nancy's condition, and immediately filed both a child abuse report and a restraining act which would keep Sue from removing Nancy from the hospital. When, after six months, Nancy was ready to be released, the hospital's attorneys filed a petition to terminate Sue's parental rights. The attorneys argued that Nancy would be best placed in a foster home or institution, rather than being given to a relative (they suspected that there was considerable violence in the homes of Nancy's grandparents and aunts and uncles).

Few would question that Nancy was an abused child. Few would question the wisdom of the hospital in taking steps to assure that Nancy would be protected from further violence and injury. The case of Sue and Nancy (not their real names, and a composite of a number of child abuse cases), is unusual. It is unusual because the intent of the parent and the cause of the injury were so obvious. It is not the normal case that a hospital child abuse diagnostic team, or a team of social workers, has clear evidence about how an injury to a child occurred. More common is the case of a child who is observed at school or in a hospital emergency room with a cut, a broken bone, or some other injury. Physical examinations, interviews with the child and the parent, and an examination of the child's medical history (if available) can sometimes help unravel the case and separate true accidents from inflicted injuries. When a child experiences violence that does not produce a black or blue mark, cut, or injury, determining whether the child has been harmed is even more complex, since variable community standards and definitions of abuse have to be applied to an act that has produced no gross visible harm.

Determining the extent of child abuse and violence toward children in the United States is a difficult task because not all cases of abuse and violence are as obvious as Nancy and Sue. Estimates of the incidence of abuse vary, as do definitions and community standards. This chapter begins by reviewing various sources of information on the extent and nature of violence and abuse toward children. Before considering who abuses children, we consider the process by which child abuse is recognized and reported in the United States. Official reports of child abuse often misrepresent who the most likely abusers are, and consequently relying on these reports leads to the perpetuation of some of the myths we discussed in Chapter 1 (e.g. only poor people abuse their children). Finally, the chapter reviews the evidence on the consequences of child abuse.

THE EXTENT OF VIOLENCE AND MALTREATMENT

Physical Punishment

Spanking children is perhaps the most common form of family violence in the United States, and because it is considered so appropriate, most people would object to calling it a case of family violence. Nevertheless, the main objective of a spanking or slapping of a child is to teach the child a lesson, to get the child to stop a certain behavior (running into the street, touching a hot stove), or to relieve a parent's own pent up frustration. As we saw in the previous chapter, many parents feel that children *need* to be hit. Justifications from a number of parents illustrate this attitude:

> I spank her once a week—when she deserves it—usually when she is eating. I believe that a child should eat so much and that is it.

> Once in a great while I use a strap. I don't believe in hitting in the head or in the face—although, Rhoda, I slapped her in her face a couple of times because she was sassing. *That* she needed.

> But right now she doesn't understand that much. I mean you can't stand and explain really something in detail that she'll understand. So a slap sometimes. She understands when she gets a slap when she's done something wrong [Gelles, 1974: 62-63].

Of course, if the slight spanking or slap does not work, the parent will typically hit a little harder, at least until the child "gets the message."

> I used to use my hand—put them over me knee and give them a good swat. But then I got myself a little paddle—the ball broke off and I kept the paddle [Gelles, 1974: 69].

Since the intent is to cause some slight harm so that the child will get the message, physical punishment, whether in the best interests of the child or not, is consistent with our definition of violence as described in Chapter 1.

Social surveys indicate that physical punishment of children is used by 84 to 97 percent of all parents at some time in their children's lives (Blumberg, 1964; Bronfenbrenner, 1958; Erlanger, 1974; Stark and McEvoy, 1970).

Despite parents' descriptions of how and why they use violence, and the claim that physical punishment is used because parents cannot reason with very young children, physical punishment of children does not cease when the children are old enough to walk, talk, or reason with. Three studies of college and university students found that half were hit when they were seniors in high school (Straus, 1971; Steinmetz, 1971; Mulligan, 1977). The most recent of these studies reported that 8 percent of the students questioned reported that they had been "physically injured" by their parents during the last year they lived at home before entering college.[1]

Child Abuse

Various techniques have been used in attempts to achieve an accurate estimate of child abuse in the United States. In 1967, David Gil (1970) conducted a nationwide inventory of reported cases of child abuse (before, however, all fifty states had enacted mandatory reporting laws). He found 6000 confirmed cases of child abuse. Gil also reported on an opinion survey that asked a representative sample of 1520 adults if they had personal knowledge of families where incidents of child abuse had occurred. Forty-five, or 3 percent of the sample, reported knowledge of forty-eight different incidents. Extrapolating this number to a national population of 110 million adults, Gil estimated that between 2.53 and 4.07 million children were abused each year, or between 13.3 and 21.4 incidents of abuse per 1000 persons in the United States. Gil's data were later analyzed by Richard Light (1974) to correct for possible instances where the same abusive incidents were known by more than one person (Light assumed that if one adult in a household knew about the incident, then other household members might also know). Light's refined estimate was that there were 500,000 abused children in the United States during the year Gil conducted his survey.

Other investigators have tried to estimate how many children are physically abused by their parents. Saad Nagi (1975) surveyed community agencies that have contact with abused children. He estimated that 167,000 cases of abuse are reported annually, while an additional 91,000 cases go unreported. Nagi estimated that there are 950,000 reportable cases of abuse *and* neglect each year—two-thirds of which are reported, and one-third of which are not. Vincent DeFrancis, then with the American Humane Association, testified before the United States Senate in 1973 and estimated that there are 30,000 to 40,000 truly abused children in the United States. Physician Vincent Fontana (1973) placed the figures as high as 1.5 million.

Two recent studies of reported child maltreatment. As you can see, there seems to be a guesstimate of the extent of child abuse for every guesser. Recently, two studies have been completed that shed some scientific light on how common abuse is. Although the studies were different in method, purpose, and findings, they do agree that abuse is considerably more common than people in the 1960s and even 1970s believed.

A national incidence study contracted by the National Center on Child Abuse and Neglect attempted to measure the national incidence of reported child maltreatment. The survey assessed how many cases were known to other investigatory agencies; Protective Service Agencies (typically the state agencies that receive the required reports of suspected child maltreatment); how many cases were known to other investigatory agencies, and how many cases were known to professionals in schools, hospitals, and other social service agencies. Table 3.1 presents the results of the national incidence survey. A total of 652,000 maltreated children were known by the agencies surveyed in the study. Stated in terms of incidence rates, it was estimated that 10.5 children are abused and/or neglected annually for each 1000 children in the United States younger than 18. Now, 10.3 per 1000 might not seem like much, but keep in mind that when statistics on crime are published, those estimates speak of incidence per 100,000 individuals. Child abuse is common enough to talk in terms of 1000 children!

A second source of data on the extent of child abuse comes from the National Study of Child Neglect and Abuse Reporting

TABLE 3.1
Estimated Number of Recognized In-Scope Children (per 1000 per year)[1]

Form of Maltreatment and Severity of Injury/Impairment	Number In-Scope Children	Incidence Rate[3] (per 1000)
Form of Maltreatment[2]		
Total, all maltreated children	652,000	10.5
Total, all abused children	351,100	5.7
Physical assault	207,600	3.4
Sexual exploitation	44,700	0.7
Emotional abuse	138,400	2.2
Total, all neglected children	329,000	5.3
Physical neglect	108,000	1.7
Educational neglect	181,500	2.9
Emotional neglect	59,400	1.0
Severity of Child's Injury/Impairment		
Fatal	1,000	0.02
Serious	136,900	2.2
Moderate	410,300	6.6
Probable	101,700	1.6

1. National incidence estimates by major form of maltreatment and by severity of maltreatment-related injury or impairments.
2. Totals may be lower than sum of categories, since a child may have experienced more than one in-scope category of maltreatment.
3. Numerator = estimated number of recognized in-scope children; denominator = 61,900, the estimated total number (in thousands) of children under 18 in the United States in December 1979.
SOURCE: Reprinted with permission from K. Burgdorf, *Recognition and Reporting of Child Maltreatment: Findings from the National Study of the Incidence and Severity of Child Abuse and Neglect,* National Center on Child Abuse and Neglect, 1980, p. 37.

conducted each year by the American Humane Association. This annual study measures the number of families, alleged perpetrators, and children involved in official reports of child maltreatment; determines the source of the reports and their geographic distribution; describes the characteristics of families involved in official reports, and identifies and describes trends in the reporting data within states (American Humane Association, 1980). The data come to the American Humane Association from the individual states.

The total number of abuse and neglect reports received in 1980 was 788,844. This constitutes a 91 percent increase in abuse

and neglect reporting since 1976. Sexual abuse was and continues to be the most rapidly increasing form of reported
maltreatment.

Of the 788,844 reports of maltreatment tabulated by the
American Humane Association, 61 percent involved children
who had experienced neglect, 20 percent involved minor injuries,
13 percent were classified as emotional maltreatment, 7 percent
were sexual maltreatment, and 4 percent of the children
experienced a major physical injury.

There are problems with both studies of reported child
maltreatment. First, definitions of maltreatment—including
physical abuse—and reporting practices vary from state to state
and from agency to agency. Each profession has a somewhat
different definition of child abuse. Second, individual, agency,
and state participation in the surveys is variable. Some states
provide complete data to the American Humane Association,
while other states do not even participate. The national survey of
cases that were known by professionals also had problems with
some agencies fully cooperating, while others failed to take part
or provided only the most meager help.

A national survey of family violence. A source of data *not
based* only on official reports or official awareness, but limited to
only one aspect of child maltreatment—physical violence—is the
survey carried out in 1976 by Murray Straus, Richard Gelles, and
Suzanne Steinmetz (1980). Straus and his colleagues conducted
a study on the subject of family violence using a nationally
representative sample of 2146 individual family members. One
part of the study focused on the 1143 homes where children
between the ages of 3 and 17 years of age lived. Parents in these
homes were asked to report on their own "conflict tactics
techniques" with their children. Among the list of conflict tactics
were eight items that dealt with physical violence. These items
ranged from pushing and shoving to the use of a knife or gun (see
Table 3.2 for a list of the violence items). The milder forms of

TABLE 3.2
Frequency of Parental Violence Toward Children

Violent Behavior	Percentage of Occurrences in Past Year				Percentage of Occurrences Ever Reported
	Once	Twice	More Than Twice	Total	
Threw something at child	1.3	1.8	2.3	5.4	9.6
Pushed, grabbed, or shoved child	4.3	9.0	18.5	31.8	46.4
Slapped or spanked child	5.2	9.4	43.6	58.2	71.0
Kicked, bit, or hit child with fist	0.7	0.8	1.7	3.2	7.7
Hit child with something	1.0	2.6	9.8	13.4	20.0
Beat up child	0.4	0.3	0.6	1.3	4.2
Threatened child with knife or gun	0.1	0.0	0.0	0.1	2.8
Used a knife or a gun on child	0.1	0.0	0.0	0.1	2.9

SOURCE: Adapted from Gelles (1980). Used by permission.

violence, were of course, the most common. However, even with severe forms of violence, the rates were surprisingly high:

- 3 percent of the parents reported that they kick, bite, or punch their child each year, while nearly 8 percent of those surveyed said they have done these acts at least once while the child was growing up.
- A little more than 1 percent of the parents said they beat their child at least once a year, while slightly more than 4 percent said they had beaten their child.
- One child in 1000 faced a parent who threatened to use a gun or a knife during the survey year.
- Nearly 3 children in 100 were threatened with a weapon by a parent while growing up. The same percentages held for children whose parents report actually using a weapon.

Straus and his colleagues also estimated the extent of abusive violence. Abusive violence was defined as acts which had a high probability of injuring the child (see Chapter 1 of this book). These included kicking, biting, punching, hitting or trying to hit a child with an object, beating up a child, and threatening or using a gun or a knife:

- Nearly 4 parents in 100 (3.8 percent) engaged in one act of abusive violence during the year prior to the survey.

Projecting this rate to all children 3 to 17 years[2] of age who lived in the home means that 1.4 million children experience acts of abusive physical violence each year.

Acts of violence not only affect a large number of children, but on average they happen more than once a year. Straus and his colleagues found that even the extreme forms of parental violence occur periodically and even regularly in the families where they occur. The median number of occurrences of acts of abusive violence was 4.5 times per year.

Straus and his colleagues' study of violence toward children confirmed previous findings that violence does not end when the children grow up. More than 80 percent of the three to nine year olds were hit at least once a year. Two-thirds of the preteens and young teenagers were hit, and more than one-third of fifteen to seventeen year olds were hit each year. Abusive acts of violence were more likely to be directed at the youngest children (three to five years of age) and the oldest (fifteen to seventeen years of age).

There are a number of limitations to the survey conducted by Straus and his associates. First, the survey measured violence toward children between the ages of three and seventeen, omitting children under three years of age, who are considered to be a high-risk population for abuse. Second, the survey included only "intact families" (because the researchers also wanted to study violence between spouses), and excluded single parents who are also believed to have higher rates of violence, abuse, and neglect. Third, the survey measured only self-reports of violence toward children. No attempt was made to measure the physical or emotional consequences of the violence. The researchers had no knowledge of how many children were actually injured. Finally, the actual measure of violence and abuse was confined to a small number of violent acts. Burning, scalding, sexual abuse, and so on, were not measured in the study.

Nevertheless, the national study did yield valuable information regarding violence toward children and a projection of a rate of child abuse that was considerably higher than previous estimates of reported physical abuse. This is quite remarkable when one considers that Straus and his colleagues used a rather restricted list of abusive violent acts.

Child Homicide

Homicide is one of the five leading causes of death for children between the ages of one and eighteen years of age. Even with an estimate this high, researchers believe that homicides of infants are probably underrecorded in health statistics (Jason et al., 1983b). Homicides may be misrecorded as accidents either because the medical examiner is unable to verify the exact cause of death or because the medical examiner wants to protect the family because of their status and position in the community. Between 1976 and 1979 there were 7026 children who were recognized as victims of homicide. Of the 178 neonates (newborns) who were killed, 66 percent were killed by a parent, 1 percent by a stepparent, and 2 percent by another family member. Infants (from one week to one year of age) were most likely to be killed by a parent (72 percent). Stepparents accounted for 2 percent of the homicides, while other family members accounted for 4 percent. The pattern changes for older children. Of the homicides of children one to seventeen years of age, 23 percent were perpetrated by parents, 3 percent by stepparents, and 6 percent by other family members (Jason et al., 1983a).

Is Child Abuse Increasing?

There is one final question that is asked when people discuss the extent of child abuse in the United States—is it increasing?

There is no question but that there has been a considerable increase in the official reporting of child abuse in the last decade. In part, this is due to the passage of mandatory reporting laws. Another contributor is the broadening of the definitions of abuse and neglect. Certainly, public awareness has been increased, and many people know more about abuse now than they did twenty or even ten years ago. Finally, cities, towns, and states have increased their own services, added hot lines or crisis lines, and have added social workers to investigate reported cases of abuse. Thus, the capacity of the system to record more cases of abuse has been increased.

Unfortunately, aside from the data on official reports of abuse, there is no way to know whether abuse has actually increased in our society. Some factors that might lead to the abuse of children (poverty, unemployment) have gotten worse in the last few years. On the other hand, other factors, such as the number of unwanted children being born, may actually have declined, limiting the number of cases of abuse. This is one question which we can only speculate about until some solid research is carried out which can go beyond relying on official report data.

WHO ARE THE ABUSERS/ WHO IS ABUSED?

There are three sources of information about who abuses children and which children are the most likely to be abused. Each source of information has specific strengths and weaknesses. Sometimes the information from each source conflicts, while other times the findings are quite consistent. To be able to appreciate the claims and findings from each source, it is important to assess the relative strengths and weaknesses of the major types of information we have on the factors associated with child abuse.

A major source of information about child abuse is clinical studies. Clinical studies depend on information collected by clinicians such as social workers, psychiatrists, psychologists, and marriage counselors. Clinicians can collect a considerable range of data with much detail because the clinicians see their patients over a period of time. However, clinical data typically are based on only a few cases (clinicians can only see a certain number of patients a week), and these cases are not randomly or representatively selected. Consequently, although data from clinical studies may be rich in descriptive information, one cannot generalize from these small numbers of cases to any larger population. Another limitation is that clinicians typically do not compare the information they obtain from cases of abuse to other families where abuse does not occur. Thus, they cannot be sure that the factors they find in the abusive families are unique to or even associated with the acts of abuse.

A second source of information about child abuse is official reports. The American Humane Association is a clearinghouse for official reports, as we mentioned in the previous section. Also, each state has its own official reporting system and records. Official reports provide information about a large number of cases and describe a wide range of cases of abuse. However, the data speak more to the factors that lead someone to get reported for abuse than to what factors are actually associated with child abuse. There is a tendency for lower income and lower social status individuals (e.g. Blacks, Spanish-speaking, ethnic minorities) to be overrepresented in these reports. Child abuse researchers have found considerable bias in the process of officially labeling and reporting child abuse. Physician Eli Newberger and his associates (1977) report that lower class and minority children seen with injuries in a private hospital are more likely than middle- and upper-class children to be labeled abused. Turbett and O'Toole (1980), using an experimental design, found that physicians are more likely to label minority children and lower-class children as abused (a mock case was presented to the physicians, with the injury remaining constant and the race or class of the child varied).

The third source of information is survey data collected from representative samples of a given population. Unfortunately, there have been very few surveys conducted on child abuse. One such study is the one conducted by Straus and associates (1980).

Our discussion of factors associated with child abuse draws from all three sources of information. Where the three sources agree we find the most powerful explanations of what child factors and parent factors are related to the abuse of children.

Child Factors

As we mentioned in the previous section, the very youngest children appear to be at the greatest risk of being abused (Fergusson et al., 1972; Gil, 1970; Johnson, 1974). Not only are young children physically more fragile and thus more susceptible to injury, but their vulnerability makes them more likely to be reported and diagnosed as abused when injured. Older children are underreported as victims of abuse. Adolescent victims may be considered delinquent or ungovernable, and thus thought of as contributing to their own victimization.

Younger boys are more likely to be abused than older boys, but the trend seems to change when the children grow up. The national survey of reported child abuse found that older girls were more likely to be victimized than younger girls.

There are other factors that raise the risk of a child being abused. Low birth weight babies (Parke and Collmer, 1975), premature children (Elmer, 1967; Newberger et al., 1977; Park and Collmer, 1975; Steele and Pollack, 1974), and handicapped, retarded, or developmentally disabled children (Freidrich and Boriskin, 1976; Gil, 1970; Steinmetz, 1978b) are all at greater risk of being abused by their parents or caretakers. In fact, any child who is considered somehow "different" seems to run a slightly greater risk of maltreatment.

Parent Factors

Individual traits. Some clinical studies suggest that parents who score low on intelligence tests are more likely to abuse their childen (Smith et al., 1973; Wright, 1971). However, most students of child abuse have found little difference between abusers and nonabusers in terms of intellectual ability.

As we discussed in the first chapter, a consistent finding in early clinical studies of abuse was that mental illness and psychosis were common among abusers. Numerous personality characteristics have been related to abuse, including depression, immaturity, and impulsiveness. However, no consistent personality profile of abusers has emerged from the years of research on child abuse, and some researchers believe that what personality factors are found, tend to be associated with being labeled an abuser rather than actually being related to abuse.

Another pervasive notion is that alcohol or drug misuse is associated with abuse (Young, 1964; Martin and Walters, 1982; Wertham, 1972; Fontana, 1973). However, other researchers note that alcohol probably plays no direct role in abuse; rather, drinking and drunkenness can be used as a socially acceptable excuse for mistreating children (Gelles, 1974; Straus et al., 1980).

A final individual factor found in abusive parents is that they tend to have unrealistically high expectations for their children. It is not uncommon for a six-month-old infant to be admitted into a hospital for injuries inflicted by a parent who was angry because the child was not toilet trained.

Demographic Factors

Clinical, official reports, and survey data find that mothers are more likely to abuse their children than fathers. Although the difference between men and women is not large, what difference does exist is probably due to factors other than gender. Mothers tend to spend more time with children, especially younger children and infants. Irrespective of the time actually spent with children, in our society mothers are considered more responsible for the children's behavior than fathers.

Young adults are more likely to abuse their children than older parents (Gil, 1970; Lauer, 1974; Straus et al., 1980; American Humane Association, 1980).

Official reports of child abuse overrepresent Blacks in comparison to the percentage of Blacks in the general population. However, other studies find that the rates of abuse among Blacks are no greater than the rates among other racial groups (Burgdorf, 1980; Straus et al., 1980). We do know that Blacks are more likely to be recognized and reported as abusers. Thus, the link between race and abuse is probably tenuous and quite limited.

Economic Factors

Clinical, official reports, and survey data are consistent in the finding that economic factors are significantly related to abuse. Low-income families have the highest rates of physical abuse and are the most likely to be reported. Those in the lowest income groups have two or three times greater rates of abuse than upper income families. Again, it is important to remember that abuse does occur in all economic groups, but it is *most likely* to happen among the poor or disadvantaged.

Since income is related to abuse, we should not be surprised that other socioeconomic factors are also related. A person's occupation has a significant impact on the chances of abuse occurring. Blue-collar workers have higher rates of the use of physical punishment and abuse (Kohn, 1977; Straus et al., 1980; Steinmetz, 1971). Children whose fathers are unemployed or work part-time are more likely to be abused compared to children of fathers with full-time jobs. There was a time when some child abuse researchers thought that working mothers were more likely to abuse their children. However, recent research finds that whether a mother works or does not work has no direct impact on her chances of abusing her child (Gelles and Hargreaves, 1981).

Stress

Given that poverty and unemployment are linked to violence toward children, it is also likely that other forms of personal and family stress are associated with violence and abuse. Stressful situations such as a new baby present, presence of a handicapped person in the home, illness, death of a family member, child care problems are all found linked to higher rates of abuse and violence. Poor housing conditions and larger than average family size are also risk factors for maltreatment of children (Gil, 1970; Straus et al., 1980; Johnson and Morse, 1968).

Social Isolation

Parents who abuse their children tend to be socially isolated from both formal and informal social networks (Elmer, 1967; Garbarino and Gilliam, 1980). Smith (1975) found that abusive mothers have fewer contacts with their parents, relatives, neighbors, or friends and engaged in few social or recreational activities. When parents are not engaged in a social network, they lack social support during times of stress. Moreover, they are less likely to change their behavior to conform with community values and standards (Steinmetz, 1978b). Thus, they are particularly vulnerable to respond violently to stress and not see this behavior as inappropriate.

The Cycle of Violence

No finding in the child abuse and violence toward children literature is more consistent than the finding that persons who observed family violence, were victims of violence, or were exposed to high levels of family violence in childhood are more likely to be abusers (Wasserman, 1967; Elmer, 1967; Straus et al., 1980). We have already provided the caution that this does not mean that all victims of childhood violence will grow up to be

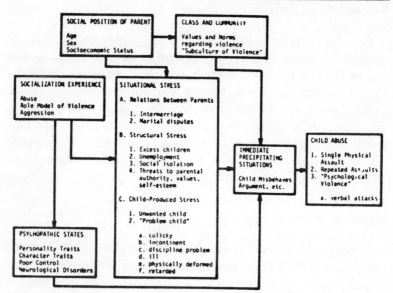

SOURCE: Gelles (1973). Reprinted with permission from the *American Journal of Orthopsychiatry*. Copyright 1973 by the American Orthopsychiatric Association, Inc.

Figure 3.1 A Social-Psychological Model of Child Abuse

abusers, nor are people who have no violence in their childhood experience immune to violent behavior as adults. But, a violent background is a significant contributor to the *likelihood* that a person will be violent toward a child.

Summary

From the preceding discussion of factors that are associated with violence toward children and child abuse, it should be quite clear that there is no single factor that leads a parent to abuse a child. Characteristics of the child, parent, family, social situation, and community are related to which children are abused and under what conditions. Figure 3.1 summarizes the factors in a social-psychological model of child abuse. This summary should not be confused with a causal explanation of violence and abuse.

Chapter 6 will review the theories and explanation of family violence in detail.

We can safely say at this point that there are multiple causes of child abuse. Since there are multiple and not single causes, this has a profound affect on the process of identifying and treating abuse. Obviously, a clinical assessment of suspected abuse cannot simply look for a single factor to signal whether a child has been abused. It is not sufficient to know that the parents were abused. An assessment of only one parent will not be sufficient; nor will just an examination of the parent's home and lifestyle. Many a social worker has misdiagnosed a suspected injury by relying too much on how neat the child's home was or was not. As we will see in the concluding chapter of this book, prevention and treatment need to be based on a model of multiple causes. The needs of the child, parents, family, and social situation are all important in understanding and helping the abusive family.

CONSEQUENCES OF CHILD ABUSE

The child abuse literature contains many assumptions about the consequences of violence and abuse for the victim, his or her family, and the society. The immediate tragic consequences are the injuries experienced by the victim. Death is another sad and tragic consequence of abuse in as many as 2000 homes a year.

The consequences of violence and abuse may extend beyond the victim and beyond the home. Some researchers believe that untreated abused children frequently grow up to be delinquents, murderers, and batterers of the next generation of children (Schmitt and Kempe, 1975).

We have repeatedly mentioned the assumptions about abuse of children leading to violent behavior when the children grow up. As adults, abused children are also thought to have higher rates of drug and alcohol abuse, criminal behavior, and psychiatric disturbances (Smith et al., 1973). Findings in the clinical literature also note that abused children who are observed in clinical and laboratory settings show signs of developmental delays and developmental difficulties (Galdston, 1975; Martin et al., 1974).

Survey research supports some of the findings from the clinical literature. A study of 4465 children and their siblings who were reported to be victims of maltreatment in eight counties in New York state, found that the maltreated children had higher rates of involvement in the juvenile justice system (Alfaro, 1977; Carr, 1977). Recent research on adolescent-to-parent violence also demonstrates that early exposure to, and experience with, violence is strongly related to the chances of a teenager using abusive violence toward a parent (Cornell and Gelles, 1982; and also see Chapter 5 of this volume).

Society also pays a price for abuse and violence toward children. Many murderers and assassins experienced violent childhoods. Arthur Bremer, who attempted to assassinate Alabama governor George Wallace, wrote in his diary, "My mother must have thought I was a canoe, she paddled me so much" (Button, 1973).

In summary, the legacy of child abuse is more than the physical scars that children carry with them. Research indicates that there are emotional and developmental scars as well. Family violence can also spill out onto the street. Moreover, there is the issue of quality of life—the day-to-day impact of violence and its threat on children and the entire family.

DISCUSSION QUESTIONS

1. What techniques have been used to measure the extent of child abuse in the United States? Discuss the advantages and disadvantages of each technique.

2. Are poor people more likely to abuse their children, to be correctly or incorrectly labeled "child abusers," or both?

3. What are the implications for clinicians who must diagnose and treat child abuse of the conclusion that there are multiple factors associated with the abuse of children?

SUGGESTED ASSIGNMENTS

1. Observe how parents discipline children in a public place. Develop a "coding" form by which you can keep track of how frequently parents use physical punishment to discipline their children. Try to observe in different locations and see whether the setting, situation, and social class of the parents influences their public behavior.

2. Contact your local child welfare agency (state, city, or local). Ask for the official tally of child abuse reports for the last ten or even twenty years. See whether you can see any trends in the changes.

NOTES

1. All the studies of college students used "convenience" or accidental samples. Questionnaires were filled out by students enrolled in introductory sociology or psychology classes. Because the samples were not representative, the results cannot be generalized to the campuses where the research was done. Because college students are not representative of all eighteen year olds, the results cannot be generalized to all high school seniors. Nevertheless, the results from three different campuses are quite consistent, and suggest that even in fairly affluent, white middle-class homes, violence toward children extends well into the children's adolescence.

2. One question frequently raised about this study is why the researchers limited their examination to children between the ages of three and seventeen. This seems odd because many people believe that the very youngest children are at the greatest risk of being abused. The answer is that a compromise had to be made in the study because one objective of the study was to study sibling violence. Children under three years of age could not be expected to rationally engage in sibling violence, so the researchers chose to look at children three years of age or older.

CHAPTER
4

The
Appropriate Victims
Women

THE SCENE IS THE EMERGENCY ROOM of a major children's hospital. This evening, like so many before, and so many that would follow, the staff is hovering over a suspected case of child abuse. A three-year-old boy is being examined. He has a number of cuts and abrasions, but what catches everyone's attention is the outline of a hand on the side of his face. A young intern suddenly turns to the boy's mother and yells at her. "How could you do this?" he begins, until he finally concludes, "I will see that your child is taken away from you and this will never happen again!"

The senior social worker on duty moves in and takes the young physician aside. Beginning with the obvious statement, "You seem to be upset," the social worker then asks the intern if he can describe the mother. "Tell me what she looks like," the social worker asks. The physician, a little calmer, could offer only the briefest description. "Come back with me," the social worker offers, and they return again to the mother and the child. "How did you lose your front teeth?" the social worker asks the mother. "Oh, my husband knocked them out last week," the mother replies in a flat, emotionless tone. Turning to the intern, the social worker notes, "You have two victims here."

Wife abuse was publically recognized as a social problem some ten years after child abuse had received widespread public attention. And yet women are still overlooked as victims of family violence, both by physicians and the public. There is no federally funded national center for wife abuse (although there was a short-lived Center on Domestic Violence in the federal government in the late 1970s). No state has passed official reporting laws for wife abuse, although many states have revised their family and criminal law to deal with wife battery. No national clearinghouse exists for collecting data on cases of wife abuse or spousal violence. Women who are abused are generally ignored or treated less seriously than child victims of family violence. Recently, when asked why the United States Senate was not holding hearings on wife abuse, as it did for child abuse, a senator replied that eliminating wife abuse "would take all the fun out of marriage." A district court judge in an eastern city, after hearing a wife present her case against her husband's violence, leaned over the bench and smiled at the husband and said, "If I were you, I would have hit her too."

As we noted in Chapter 2, there are abundant historical and cross-cultural data to support the claim that women are the "appropriate victims" of domestic violence. In fact, some researchers have gone so far as to claim that the "marriage license is a hitting license." Lately, we have learned that it does not take a license to hit. This chapter begins by reviewing some of the newest research in the field of family violence, the study of courtship or dating violence. Next, we consider the extent of violence toward wives and what factors are associated with wife battery. The following section takes on the most pervasive myth in the study of wife abuse; if women stay with their assaultive husbands, then they, the women, must like the violence. In this section we review the reasons why some women stay in violent relationships and why others leave. We also examine a new study that looks at women who stayed with their husbands and got their husbands to stop the violence. Finally, the chapter concludes with a discussion of husbands as victims of domestic violence.

COURTSHIP VIOLENCE

The virtues of romantic love, a phenomenon considered synonymous with American dating patterns, have been extolled in poems, songs, romance novels, television soap operas, and folklore. Sadly, along with the moonlight cruises, the first kiss, the flirtations and affections is also the startling fact that violence is very much a part of American dating patterns. New studies which examined the possibility of violence in dating and courtship found that *between 22 percent and 67 percent of dating relationships involve violence* (Cate et al., 1982; Henton et al., 1983; Laner et al., 1981; Makepiece, 1981; 1983). As with other forms of intimate violence, the milder forms of violence (pushing, slapping, shoving) are the most common. However, severe violence is surprisingly common. Oregon State University sociologist Rodney Cate and his colleagues (1982) found that *38 percent of their unmarried college-aged respondents had experienced kicking, biting, or being hit with a fist.* This violence also is a pattern among couples of high school age. *Twelve percent of high school daters reported experiencing a form of dating violence* (Henton et al., 1983). *One victim reported having a gun or knife used on her, while two persons said they used a gun or a knife on a dating partner.*

Perhaps the saddest and most revealing finding from the research on dating violence is how the individuals perceive the violence. In a study conducted by the sociologist June Henton and her colleagues (1983), *more than one-fourth of the victims, and three of ten offenders, interpreted the violence as a sign of love.* This is a scary extension of the elementary school-yard scenario where the young girl recipient of a push, shove, or hit, thinks that it means the boy who hit her likes her.

Perhaps the biggest surprise from the research on dating violence is that rather than the violent episodes shattering the romantic images held by the participants, one gets the impression that violence serves to protect the romantic illusions of dating. Victims of dating violence were likely to take the blame for helping to start the violence and were reluctant to blame their partners for the abuse. In addition, victims of courtship violence were reluctant to tell others about their experiences. If they did talk about the violence, it was with peers and not parents or teachers.

It is quite clear from the new studies of courtship violence that many of the patterns we find in marital violence emerge long before a person gets married. If the marriage license is not a hitting license, then we must focus more closely on the relationship between romance, intimacy, and violence.

EXTENT OF MARITAL VIOLENCE

The pattern of courtship violence helps us to understand some important things about marital violence. First, as we have noted previously, there is a tendency on the part of many victims and offenders to view the violence as appropriate. Second, female victims are reluctant to blame their partners for the violence and tend to say that both persons were to blame for the abuse. Third, victims might blame themselves ("I asked for it"). Last, there is a tendency not to talk about the violence with family or friends.

Because violence between husbands and wives was traditionally hidden in the home, there has been a general lack of awareness of the seriousness and extent of the problem. Unlike child abuse, no official federal or state agencies are mandated or contracted to record the incidence of spouse abuse. Whereas mandatory reporting laws for child abuse and neglect were enacted in the late 1960s and early 1970s, no mandatory reporting laws exist for spouse violence. Some hospitals record the number of women treated for spousal violence, and most police departments keep a rough record of domestic disturbance calls. Even without official records on spouse abuse, a variety of data sources suggest that spouse violence is far more extensive than commonly realized.

Homicide

Homicide is the one aspect of spousal violence on which official data are available. Researchers generally report that intrafamilial homicides account for between 20 percent and 40 percent of all murders (Curtis, 1974). In 1979, 844 husbands were killed by their wives, while 1009 wives were slain by their husbands (Uniform Crime Reports, 1980).

Criminal Assault

In one study, aggravated assault between husbands and wives made up 11 percent of all reported criminal assaults (Pittman and Handy, 1964). In another report, husband-wife assault constituted 52 percent of all assaults in Detroit (Boudouris, 1971). Because so many assaults are recorded as domestic disturbance calls, police reports surely underestimate the proportion of all assaults that are intrafamilial.

Applicants for Divorce

Studies of couples applying for divorce also provide some information on the extent of husband-wife violence. The psychologist George Levinger (1966) discovered that 22 percent of the middle-class and 40 percent of the working-class applicants for divorce whom he interviewed discussed "physical violence" as a major complaint. John O'Brien (1971) reports that 17 percent of the couples he interviewed spontaneously mentioned violent behavior in their marriages.

National Crime Survey Report

Another source of information on the extent and patterns of domestic violence is the National Crime Survey, conducted by the U.S. Justice Department. This survey estimates the amount of crime committed both against persons aged twelve and older and against households. The chief advantage of the National Crime Survey is that it investigates the occurrence of crime whether it is reported to the authorities or not (the Uniform Crime Reports cited above measures only crimes reported to the police). The published results of this survey, *Intimate Victims: A Study of Violence Among Friends and Relatives* (U.S. Department of Justice, 1980), reported on events occurring between 1973 and 1976 as derived from the interviews conducted twice a year with approximately 136,000 occupants of a representative sample of some 60,000 housing units in the United States.

The major results of the National Crime Survey were:

- There were about 3.8 million incidents of violence among intimates in the four-year period of the survey. Nearly a third were committed by offenders related to the victims.
- An analysis of single offender incidents revealed 1,055,000 incidents between relatives. Of this number, 616,000 (58 percent) were between spouses or ex-spouses.

A National Survey of Marital Violence

Although each of the pieces of information mentioned above offers a clue to the actual level of marital violence, the studies have numerous methodological flaws. Like the research on child abuse discussed in the previous chapter, studies of wife abuse and spousal violence frequently rely on small, nonrepresentative samples or the use of official data (e.g. police calls). It is impossible to generalize from these studies to marriage in the United States. The National Crime Victim survey failed to employ a precise measure of violence, and thus the results are rather difficult to interpret.

The same national study that examined child abuse (see the previous chapter) also examined marital violence. Murray Straus and his colleagues interviewed a nationally representative sample of 2143 family members. Again, using the same Conflict Tactics Scale, the researchers examined violence between husbands and wives.

- In 16 percent of the homes surveyed, some kind of violence between spouses had occurred in the year of the survey. More than one in four (28 percent) of the couples reported marital violence at some point in their marriages.

As with violence toward children and courtship violence, the milder forms of violence were the most common (see Table 4.1):

- In terms of those acts of violence that would be considered wife beating (that is, had the high potential of causing an injury), the national family violence survey revealed that 3.8 percent of American women, or one woman in twenty-two, was a victim of abusive violence during the twelve-month period prior to the interview.

Wife beating is an unfortunate pattern, not a single event in most violent households. On average, a woman who is a victim of wife abuse is abused three times each year.

TABLE 4.1
Frequency of Marital Violence:
Comparison of Husband and Wife Violence Rates
(in percentages)

| | Incidence Rate | | | Frequency* | | |
| | | | Mean | | Median | |
	H	W	H	W	H	W
Wife-Beating and Husband-Beating (N to R)	3.8	4.6	8.0	8.9	2.4	3.0
Overall Violence Index (K to R)	12.1	11.6	8.8	10.1	2.5	3.0
K. Threw something at spouse	2.8	5.2	5.5	4.5	2.2	2.0
L. Pushed, grabbed, shoved spouse	10.7	8.3	4.2	4.6	2.0	2.1
M. Slapped spouse	5.1	4.6	4.2	3.5	1.6	1.9
N. Kicked, bit, or hit with fist	2.4	3.1	4.8	4.6	1.9	2.3
O. Hit or tried to hit with something	2.2	3.0	4.5	7.4	2.0	3.8
P. Beat up spouse	1.1	0.6	5.5	3.9	1.7	1.4
Q. Threatened with knife or gun	0.4	0.6	4.6	3.1	1.8	2.0
R. Used a knife or gun	0.3	0.2	5.3	1.8	1.5	1.5

SOURCE: From Murray A. Straus, "Wife-Beating: How Common and Why?" *Victimology*, 1978, 2(3/4), p. 44 © 1978 Visage Press Inc. All rights reserved.

A Note on Marital Rape

Just as violence is not the only form of abuse children experience, physical abuse is not the only form of victimization wives endure. The sociologist Diana Russell (1980) interviewed a representative sample of 930 women in San Francisco. Of the 644 married women in the sample, 12 percent said they had been raped by their own husbands. The sociologists David Finkelhor and Kirsti Yllo (1982) asked a random sample of women, "Has your spouse (or a person you are living with as a couple) ever used physical force or threat to try to have sex with you?" Of the women, 10 percent said "yes." Although most states prohibit a wife from charging her husband with rape, these two studies produce the same remarkable finding: One of the most common forms of sexual victimization for a woman is to be forced into having sex or engaging in a sex act she objects to, by her husband. Russell found that twice as many women in her sample had been raped by their husbands as by strangers. Even these statistics are low, because many women do not see forced sex with a husband as rape.

FACTORS ASSOCIATED WITH WIFE ABUSE

The earliest publications on the subject of wife abuse took a distinctively psychiatric view of both offender and victim. Women who were abused were believed to suffer from psychological disorders as did the men who abused them. Research conducted in the 1970s and 1980s found this view of wife battery too simplistic. There are a number of individual, demographic, relational, and situational factors related to violence toward wives. These factors are probably all interrelated. For example, certain relationship patterns are probably more common in certain social classes than others.

Individual Factors

Batterers. Men who assault and batter their wives have been found to have low self-esteem and vulnerable self-concepts. A remark, insult, or comment that might not affect someone else may be interpreted as a slight, insult, or challenge to many of these men. Abusive men have also been described as feeling helpless, powerless, and inadequate (Ball, 1977; Weitzman and Dreen, 1982). Violence is frequently used as a means of trying to demonstrate one's power and adequacy.

Abused women. Psychological portraits of battered wives are difficult to interpret. One never really knows whether the personality factors found in battered wives were present before they were battered or are the result of the victimization. As with other studies of family violence, personality studies of battered women frequently use small samples, clinical samples, and often fail to have comparison groups. Thus, generalizing from these studies is difficult, and demonstrating that battered women are actually different from nonvictimized women is nearly impossible using these data.

Battered women have been described as dependent, having low esteem, and feeling inadequate and helpless (Ball, 1977; Shainess, 1977; Walker, 1979). Sometimes the personality profiles of battered women reported in the literature seem directly opposite. While some researchers describe battered women as unassertive, shy, and reserved (Weitzman and Dreen, 1982), other reports picture battered women as aggressive, masculine, frigid, and masochistic (Snell et al., 1964; Ball, 1977).

It is best to be wary of psychological profiles of battered women. In addition to small samples and no comparison groups, samples of battered women are frequently drawn only from battered wife shelters. Thus, the researchers are studying only one type of battered woman, one who seeks help, and it is certainly unrealistic to generalize from these women to all battered women.

Alcohol. Studies of marital violence typically find a relationship between alcohol use and abuse and domestic violence. Various studies note that between 36 and 52 percent of wife batterers also abuse alcohol (Brekke and Saunders, 1982). Virtually every study of wife abuse conducted notes the close link between alcohol and violence.

That alcohol is related to wife abuse is clear. What is not clear is how alcohol is related to violence. Do men drink, lose control, and then abuse? Or, does alcohol become a convenient excuse or rationalization for violent behavior? Cross-cultural studies of alcohol use and studies of marital violence suggest that alcohol itself does not lead to violence; rather, men drink (or say they drink) to have a socially acceptable excuse for violent behavior (Gelles, 1974).

Demographic Factors

Results of the National Family Violence survey indicate that all forms of marital violence occur most frequently among those under thirty years of age (Straus et al., 1980). The rate of marital violence among those under thirty years of age is more than double the rate for the next older age group (thirty-one to fifty).

Studies that examine women who seek help from agencies or shelters also find that the mean age is thirty or younger (Gayford, 1975; Fagan et al., 1983).

Straus and his colleagues also found that wife abuse was more common in Black households than white households. This is different from child abuse where there were no major differences between Blacks and whites. Obviously, race is not the only factor in play here. Income and occupational status are probably also associated with the increased rates of wife abuse among Blacks.

Marital violence can occur at any stage of a marriage, but as the data on age would appear to indicate, newer marriages have the highest risk of wife abuse. Maria Roy found that the highest percentage of battered women were married from 2.5 to 5 years (1977). Another study reported that the median length of a violent marriage was 5 years (Fagan et al., 1983).

Economic Factors

Irrespective of the method, sample, or research design, studies of marital violence support the hypothesis that spousal violence is more likely to occur in low-income, low-socioeconomic-status families. These findings do not mean that wife abuse is confined only to low-income, low-status families. One woman who was married to a Fortune 500 corporate executive described how her husband beat her and how, in order to escape his violence, she slept in their Continental Mark IV every Saturday night. A good deal of violence in middle- and upper-class families is kept secret. Neighbors do not live close by, and do not call the police. Upper-class husbands seem to have more success in keeping the police from arresting them. Nevertheless, it would appear that the probability of wife abuse occurring in high income, upper-class homes is less than the probability of occurrence among the poor.

One of the main factors associated with wife battery is the employment status of the husband. Being unemployed is devastating to men in our society. It is a clear demonstration that they are not fulfilling society's expectation that men are the family providers. Unemployed men have rates of wife assault that are almost double the rates for employed men (Rounsaville, 1978; Gayford, 1975, Prescott and Letko, 1977). Men who are employed part-time have even higher rates, probably because they have the worst of all possible worlds—no full-time job and not eligible for unemployment or other benefits (Straus et al., 1980).

The Cycle of Violence

As with child battering, wife battering is related to experiences with violence. Individuals who have experienced violent childhoods are more likely to grow up and assault their wives than men who have not experienced childhood violence. Physician J. J. Gayford (1975) as well as other investigators found that both offender *and* victim had violence-ridden childhoods (Roy, 1977; Fagan et al., 1983).

Again, it is very important to introduce the caution that a violent background does not predetermine a violent adulthood. Although the chances of being an offender and victim are increased if one grows up in a violent home, there are many violent people who had limited exposure to violence as children, and some people who experienced extremely violent childhoods grow up to be nonviolent.

Relationship Factors

One of the most compelling indicators that domestic violence is not purely a product of individual factors is the finding that certain properties of marital relations raise the likelihood of violence. That structural properties of marriage and family life are involved means that abuse can not be solely attributed to "bad" or "sick" people.

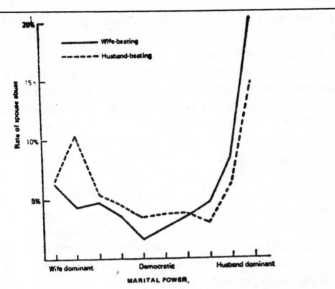

SOURCE: From Murray Straus, Richard J. Gelles, and Suzanne K. Steinmetz, *Behind Closed Doors: Violence in the American Family.* Achor/Doubleday, p. 194.

Figure 4.1 Marital Violence by Marital Power

Early studies of spousal violence found that men whose educational attainment and occupational status was lower than their wives were more likely to assault their wives than men who were better educated and had better jobs than their spouses (Gelles, 1974; O'Brien, 1971). Additional research bears out the hypothesis that status inconsistency and status incompatability are related to marital violence. One example of status inconsistency is where a husband's educational background is considerably higher than his occupational attainment (e.g. a Ph.D. who drives a taxi cab). Status incompatability is when the husband, who society expects to be the leader of the family, has less education and a poorer job than his wife. In both of these cases, the risk of marital violence is elevated (Hornung et al., 1981; Steinmetz, 1982; Rounsaville, 1978).

Decision-making patterns or power balance was also found to be related to domestic violence. Democratic households—homes where the decision making is shared—are the least violent families (see Figure 4.1). Homes where all the decisions are made either by the wife or the husband have the highest rates of violence.

A final relationship factor is that if there is one type of family violence in a home, there is a good chance that another form of violence will be present. Child abuse rates are higher in homes where there is spouse abuse (Straus et al., 1980; Hilberman and Munson, 1977; Finklehor, 1983).

Stress and Isolation

Social stress and social isolation are two final factors that are strongly related to the risk of wife-abuse. Unemployment, financial problems, sexual difficulties, low job satisfaction, large family size, and poor housing conditions are all related to marital violence. The more socially isolated a family is, the higher the risk that there will be wife-abuse.

STAYING IN OR LEAVING BATTERING RELATIONSHIPS

One thing is quite clear from the review of research of wife-abuse—violence in marital relationships is not a one-shot affair, but, rather, it is a pattern that endures over a considerable period of time. Because marital violence is a recurrent behavior, and because the victims—women—are adults and not helpless children, some people have assumed that the solution to marital violence is for the battered women to leave or divorce their husbands. We noted in Chapter 1 that one of the most pervasive myths in the field of family violence is the myth that battered wives like being hit, otherwise they would leave. Considerable research has been conducted that refutes the myth of the masochistic battered wife. In general the studies find that many factors—economic, relational, cultural, and social—constrain women from leaving a battering relationship.

Psychologist Lenore Walker (1979) has examined numerous cases of battered women and has developed the theory of "learned helplessness" to explain why so many women endure such extreme violence for so long. Walker notes that women who experience repeated physical assaults at the hands of their husbands have much lower self-concepts than women whose marriages were free from violence. Walker postulates that the repeated beatings and lower self-concepts leave women with the feeling that they cannot control what will happen to them. They feel they are unable to protect themselves from further assaults and feel incapable of controlling the events that go on around them. Thus, like laboratory animals, which, after experiencing repeated shocks from which there is no apparent escape, battered women eventually learn that they are helpless to prevent violent attacks.

"Learned helplessness" implies a rather passive nature of battered women, and it is important not to confuse the situation of women who are battered with the situation of the laboratory animals from whom the theory of "learned helplessness" was derived. Most battered women are far from passive. They call the police, they go to social workers or mental health agencies, they flee to shelters or the homes of friends or parents. But, in many ways, women are constrained by social forces from leaving a violent relationship. Legal writer Elizabeth Truninger (1971) lists seven factors that help explain why women do not break off relationships with abusive husbands: (1) they (the women) have negative self-concepts; (2) they believe their husbands will reform; (3) economic hardship; (4) they have children who need a father's economic support; (5) they doubt they can get along alone; (6) they believe divorcees are stigmatized; and (7) it is difficult for women with children to get work.

In our own research we compared battered women who stayed with their violent husbands to women who called the police, sought a divorce, or went to a mental health agency for help. We found that certain factors distinguished women who stayed in the violent relationship from women who sought help or left a violent husband. First, those women who leave seem to experience the most severe and frequent violence. Second, women who experienced more violence as children were more likely to remain in violent relationships. In addition, women with limited educational attainment and occupational skills were more likely to stay with battering husbands. The fewer resources a woman had, the less power she had, the more she was entrapped in a marriage and the more she suffered at the hands of her husband (Gelles, 1976).

We also found that women did not suffer in silence. A good number did seek outside help, but found this help to be of rather limited value. Police intervention is frequently ineffective. Social service agencies often cannot offer much help other than the names of battered wife shelters, and the courts lack understanding of domestic violence and also lack the ability rapidly and effectively to protect battered women.

Sociologist Millie Pagelow (1981) has also investigated the situation of battered women. Her research on women who sought help from shelters confirms some of our findings while other findings are not supported in Pagelow's study. Pagelow administered questionnaires to 350 women who had sought temporary residence for themselves or their children in battered wife shelters. Severity and frequency of violence did not influence the decision of whether to leave or not. While some of the women in the shelters endured years of violence and abuse, others fled after the first or second incident. Also, Pagelow did not find support for the association between violence experienced as a child and the decision to stay or leave. Actually, shelter residents who experienced childhood violence were more apt to leave after the first incident of violence or else they remained in a violent home a shorter time than other women. Pagelow did find that the resources women had (educational, occupation, income) did influence whether they stayed or left a violent husband.

One reason for the different findings is that Pagelow used very different samples of women than we did. We studied women who were not in shelters, while she gathered data from shelter residents. Also, Pagelow did not use a comparison group—she had no groups of women who had stayed with their husbands. Thus her conclusions about staying or leaving can be made only tentatively, since she did not actually study women who stayed.

In contrast to Pagelow's study of women who leave their husbands, the sociologist Lee Bowker examined the stories and situations of women who chose to stay with their husbands and get them to stop being violent. Bowker (1983) conducted 136 in-depth interviews over a nine-month period with women who stayed with their husbands and succeeded in getting their husbands to stop using violence. Bowker used a variety of strategies to locate these women—referrals from social service agencies, radio and television appearances by members of the research team, newspaper advertisements, and so on.

Bowker learned that the techniques used by women to get their husbands to stop using violence clustered into three types: (1) personal strategies, including talking, promising, threatening, hiding, passive defense, aggressive defense, and avoidance; (2) use of informal help sources, including family members, in-laws, neighbors, friends, and shelters; and, (3) formal help sources, including the police, social service agencies, and lawyers and district attorneys. The most common personal strategy was passive defense-—covering one's body with arms, hands, or feet. The most common informal strategy were friends; social services were the leading formal source of help.

Which technique worked best? There was no simple answer. Bowker reports that no single strategy is guaranteed to stop violence, but almost any strategy or help-source can ultimately work. What matters is "the woman's showing her determination that the violence must stop now."

A NOTE ON HUSBANDS AS VICTIMS

The results of the National Family Violence Survey (summarized in Table 4.1) included data on violence toward husbands. A little more than 4 percent (4.6 percent) of the wives surveyed reported that they had engaged in violence toward their husbands that could be considered abusive (Straus et al., 1980). Violence toward husbands, or "husband abuse," has been a controversial area in the study of domestic violence. There has been consider-able rhetoric on this topic, but, unfortunately, precious little scientific data.

In 1978, the sociologist Suzanne Steinmetz published an article designed to demonstrate that husbands as well as wives were the victims of violence in the home. Steinmetz reviewed numerous investigations of family violence and found, contrary to some feminist and scholarly claims, women were not the *only* victims of family violence. Steinmetz went on to claim that it was husband and *not* wife abuse that was the most underreported form of family violence. Steinmetz was immediately challenged and attacked by feminists and scholars alike for misreading, misinterpreting, and misrepresenting her findings (see Pleck et al., 1978).

Unlike most debates among scholars, this one spilled over into the public media (*Time, the Today Show, The Phil Donohue Show, The David Susskind Show*) and even into the syndicated column of Ann Landers (for a detailed discussion of the public debate, see Jones, 1980). Sadly, the debate boiled in the public domain, but the issue received virtually no attention in the scholarly arena. There have been only a few scholarly articles on violence towards husbands published since Steinmetz's article in 1978.

It is quite clear that men are struck by their wives. It is also clear that because men are typically larger than their wives and usually have more social resources at their command, that they do not have as much physical or social damage inflicted on them as is inflicted on women. Data from studies of households where the police intervened in domestic violence, clearly indicate that men are rarely the victims of "battery" (Berk et al., 1983). Thus, although the data in Table 4.1 show similar rates of hitting, when injury is considered, marital violence is primarily a problem of victimized women.

DISCUSSION QUESTIONS

1. Compare the nature of courtship violence to violence within marriage. Is the marriage license a hitting license or are there other factors that increase the risk that intimates will be violent toward one another?

2. Discuss the various ways economic factors influence the chances that spouse abuse will occur.

3. Why is it unfair to "blame" battered women for remaining with their battering spouses? What resources or facilities in the community could help women who wanted to leave their violent husbands?

4. Are there battered husbands?

SUGGESTED ASSIGNMENTS

1. Identify the services that exist for battered women in your community (e.g. shelters or safe houses; hot lines; counseling groups for battered women, and so on).

2. Talk to someone who works in a shelter or a safe house. Is the address of the shelter public or a secret? How many women and children can the shelter hold? Does the shelter ever turn away women? Why? What is the philosophy of the shelter—how do they approach the problem of violence toward women?

3. Create a resource book for victims of spouse abuse in your community—include the names, addresses, and telephone numbers of all resources that could be used by victims of spouse abuse.

4. Find out what services (if any) are available for victims of courtship violence at your college or university.

Hidden Victims

Siblings, Adolescents, Parents, and the Elderly

THE INCREASING PUBLIC and professional attention paid to child and wife abuse has had the unanticipated consequence of leading many people to believe that violence toward women and children is the most common and most problematic aspect of violence in the home. Yet, children and women are not the only victims of family violence. In fact, they are not the most commonly victimized family members—siblings are.

This chapter examines violent family relations that have been largely overlooked by the public, researchers, and members of the social service and public policy communities. Each form of violence has been overlooked for a slightly different reason. Violence between siblings is so common that people rarely think of these events as family violence. We have already mentioned adolescent victims of family violence when we discussed violence toward children (see Chapter 3). Discussions of child abuse rarely extend beyond the youngest victims. Older victims of parental violence tend to be blamed for their own victimization. Teenagers are thought of as causing their own victimization, and as we blame the victim, we tend to overlook this violent family relationship. Parent abuse is considered almost humorous by those who first hear of it. Researchers who study parent abuse have been teased that they must be running out of victims, or asked if "pet abuse" is next on their list. The large majority of parent victims are so shamed by their victimization that they are reluctant to discuss anything but the most severe incidents; and, when they do report, they, like adolescent victims, are blamed for being hit. Finally, the elderly are victims of intimate violence. They may truly be the hidden victims, since one of the unfortunate aspects of aging in our society is the removal of the elderly from their regular and normal systems of social interaction (e.g. work).

Although research on each of these types of family violence is scarce, any book on family violence would be incomplete without a discussion of violent relations other than parent to child and between husband and wife.

SIBLING VIOLENCE

Normative Attitudes Toward Sibling Violence

Sibling violence is the most common form of family violence. Siblings hitting one another is so common that few people consider these behaviors violent. The existence of social norms that encourage expressions of aggressive behavior among siblings hinders the recognition of sibling violence as abnormal and worthy of serious concern. Most parents view conflict among siblings as an inevitable part of growing up and rarely discourage expressions of aggressive behavior between their offspring.

Sociologists who have studied violence between brothers and sisters have found that parents feel it is important for their children to learn how to handle themselves in violent situations. Parents do not actively discourage their children from becoming involved in disputes with their siblings. In fact, parents may try to ignore aggressive interactions and only become involved when minor situations are perceived as escalating into major confrontations. Sibling rivalry is considered a "normal" part of relations between brothers and sisters, and many parents believe that such rivalry provides a good training ground for the successful management of aggressive behavior in the real world. American parents generally feel that some exposure to aggression is a positive experience that should occur early in life. Seven out of ten Americans agreed with the statement: "When a boy is growing up it is important for him to have a few fist fights" (Stark and McEvoy, 1970). And, the better prepared children are to defend themselves from a sibling, the better prepared they will be for conflicts with classmates and friends.

The sociologist Suzanne Steinmetz (1977), in her study of sibling conflict in a representative sample of 57 intact families in Delaware, found that it was sometimes difficult to get parents to discuss sibling violence, not because they were ashamed or embarrassed to admit such behavior, but because the parents often did not view their children's actions as abusive and worthy of mentioning. When questioned further about particular incidents, parents said that they found their children's conduct to be annoying but they did not perceive the situation as one of conflict. When prompted, parents will freely discuss or admit to the existence of sibling violence in their homes. Parents willingly tell friends, neighbors, and researchers, without embarrassment or restraint, how their children are constantly involved in argumentative and abusive behavior toward one another. When Steinmetz asked the parents in her study: "How do your children get along," she received such statements as:

> Terrible! They fight all the time.
>
> Oh it's just constant, but I understand that this is normal.
>
> I talk to other people and their children are the same way [Steinmetz, 1977: 43].

From these typical comments, it becomes obvious that parents view such frequent and violent confrontations as inevitable.

Perhaps parents may be somewhat justified in their assessment of the inevitability of sibling violence. The existence of sibling rivalry has been documented throughout history. Researchers, pointing to the historical existence of sibling rivalry, refer to the Biblical story of Cain and Abel, in which Cain kills his brother (Sargent, 1962; Straus et al., 1980). This is perhaps the earliest, although certainly not the only, recorded account of sibling violence. Evidence of violence between brothers and sisters can also be found in more contemporary sources. However, what is lacking in the recorded accounts of sibling violence is information from controlled, scientific research projects. Sociologists Suzanne Steinmetz and Murray Straus report that prior to their own investigations into the causes, frequency and patterns of sibling violence, information on noninfant, nonfatal sibling violence was almost nonexistent.

Those research articles that did appear in the scientific literature prior to 1977 dealt almost exclusively with sibling murders (Adelson, 1972; Bender, 1959; Sargent, 1962; Smith, 1965). Society appears only to take notice of the most extreme expressions of sibling violence. Levels of violence among siblings that do not exceed the levels defined as socially acceptable or "normal" go unnoticed by both researchers and society in general. This historic acceptance of sibling violence as normal and inevitable has made it difficult to establish if the rates of sibling violence have increased, decreased, or remained the same. Base line data simply do not exist. Even today, after the completion of a few studies on sibling violence, the level of awareness concerning sibling violence as a significant form of family violence is low.

The Extent of Violence Between Siblings

Steinmetz's (1977) previously mentioned investigation into sibling rivalry discovered frequent occurrences of sibling conflict in American families. The parents in 49 families recorded the frequency and types of violent behavior occurring between their offspring during a one-week period. Steinmetz reported that a total of 131 sibling conflicts occurred during this period, ranging from short-lived arguments to more serious confrontations. She believes, however, that this figure, although high, is probably a considerable underestimation of the true extent of sibling aggression. She notes that there are many problems inherent in relying upon parents to record the frequency of sibling conflicts. For example, in most of the families in Steinmetz's sample both parents worked, reducing the amount of time the parents actually spent with their children. This in turn reduced the opportunity of parents to observe and record violent behaviors between children. Steinmetz also found that often parents would record a series of events as one incident since the events were all related to the same causal event. The way in which parents chose to record conflicts eventually affected the total number of conflicts observed. Finally, parents were at times too busy to record their children's behavior. Recording the violent incidents at a later time increased the probability that some occurrences of sibling conflict could have been forgotten. Regardless of the shortcomings in the recording technique, Steinmetz was able to demonstrate that sibling violence was occurring and the frequency of occurrences appeared to be quite high.

Several years later, a team of sociologists (Straus, Gelles, and Steinmetz, 1980) conducted a nationally representative study on family violence. Sibling violence was one of several forms of family violence investigated. They reported the startling statistic that four out of five children between the ages of three and seventeen, residing in the United States, and having one or more siblings living at home, engaged in at least one violent act toward a sibling during a one-year period. This translates into approximately 36.3 million children being violent toward a sibling within a year's time. Much of the violence that siblings engage in includes pushing, slapping, shoving, and throwing things. Some people have argued that these behaviors are not really serious and serve to overestimate the real rates of sibling violence. Therefore, when these "lesser" forms of violence are excluded and the researchers examine only the more severe forms of violence (such as kicking, biting, pushing, hitting with an object, and "beating up"), the rates are still alarmingly high. Straus and his colleagues estimate that over 19 million children a year engage in acts of abusive violence against a sibling.

Factors Related to Sibling Violence

Sex. Given that sibling violence occurs with alarming frequency, the question is raised as to whether all children engage in these violent acts with the same frequency or if these aggressive actions are being carried out by a particular category of children. While children of all ages and both sexes engage in violence and abuse against a brother or sister, there appears to be some difference in the rates at which they are violent. A commonly held

TABLE 5.1
Percentage of Incidents of Hidden Forms of Family Violence

Violent Acts	Sibling to Sibling	Parent to Adolescent	Adolescent to Parent
Any violence	82	46	9
Pushed or shoved	74	25	6
Slapped	48	28	3
Threw things	43	4	4
Kicked, bit, punched	42	2	2
Hit with object	40	7	2
Beat up	16	1.3	0.7
Threatened with a knife or gun	0.8	0.2	0.3
Used a knife or gun	0.3	0.2	0.2

Based on data collected by Straus, Gelles, and Steinmetz (1980).

belief in our society is that boys are more physically aggressive and girls are more verbally aggressive. One would expect then that sibling violence is initiated primarily by brothers. Although the research on sibling violence tends to support this common sense belief, the support is not as overwhelming as one might expect (Straus et al., 1980). While 83 percent of boys were aggressive toward a brother or sister, so were 74 percent of girls! At all ages girls were less violent than boys, but the difference was relatively small.

Age. Research into sibling violence also confirms the belief that as children grow older, the rates of using violence to resolve conflicts between siblings decrease (Steinmetz, 1977; Straus et al., 1980). This could be the result of children becoming better equipped at using verbal skills to settle disputes. Also, as children grow older, they spend less and less time in each other's company. Older children spend more time away from home and away from potential sibling conflicts.

Steinmetz found that the factors precipitating conflicts varied with age. Younger children were more likely to have conflicts centered around possessions, especially toys. One family in Steinmetz's sample reported that, during a one-week period, their young children fought over "the use of a glider, sharing a truck, sharing a tricycle, knocking down one child's building blocks and taking them." Young adolescent conflicts focused on territory, with adolescents becoming very upset if a sibling invaded their personal space. "They fuss. They say, 'He's sitting in my seat,' or 'He has got an inch of his pants on the line where I am supposed to be'" (Steinmetz, 1977: 53). One father, driven to the breaking point by his children constantly fighting in the back seat of the car, took a can of red paint and painted boundary lines on the back seat and floor in an attempt to end disputes over personal space. Teenage conflicts, although less in number, still exist. These conflicts centered around responsibilities, obligations, and social awareness. Teenagers were more likely to be verbally aggressive and found that hollering was usually effective in conflict situations, especially when the siblings differed in opinions.

Other factors. Little is known about the factors that may be potentially associated with sibling violence. Those who have studied sibling murder often attribute the cause of such extreme aggression to jealousy. Dr. Adelson, after examining several children who had committed murder, concluded that pre-schoolers are capable of homicidal rage when they are threatened regarding their sense of security in the family unit. However, it has not yet been established if lesser forms of sibling aggression can be attributed to the same factors believed to be associated with murder.

Research on violent adolescents generally concludes that the factors associated with intimate adult violence (child abuse and spouse abuse) are of little use in helping to explain violence among children (Cornell and Gelles, 1982). In other words, children are not commiting acts of violence for the same reason as adults.

Finally, some researchers have postulated that sibling violence is a learned response. Although it is commonly believed that children will resort to violence as a natural way to resolve conflicts, the sociologists Straus, Gelles, and Steinmetz (1980) believe that siblings learn from their parents that physical punishment is an appropriate technique for resolving conflicts. Children raised in nonviolent environments learn there are a variety of nonviolent techniques available for resolving conflicts with brothers and sisters and later with their spouses and children.

VIOLENCE TOWARD ADOLESCENTS

Although young children are the most frequent targets of physical abuse, abuse is *not* limited to very young children (see Chapter 3). Preteens and teenagers are experiencing a wide range of violent treatments at the hands of their parents. While it is true that the rates of physical violence and abuse decline as children grow older, researchers who have examined the rates of adolescent victimization were surprised at the number of teenagers being mistreated in American families. Societal attitudes perpetuate the myth that adolescents are rarely abused by their parents since they acquire greater physical strength with age. Parents may begin to fear retaliation at the hands of children whose physical strength may surpass their own. For those children who are being struck, many people believe they precipitate or deserve being hit. Common sense sometimes suggests that teenagers frustrate their parents to such an extent that they deserve what they get!

The status of adolescents in our society is much the same as that of younger children. Both are considered the property and responsibility of their parents. Parents are granted societal permission to engage in a wide range of behaviors when disciplining their offspring. Although parents are expected to practice restraint when disciplining, the use of physical punishment is sanctioned as an acceptable behavior even for teenage children. Both young children and adolescents are relegated to a subordinate position within the family structure with parents being granted the right to bestow rewards and punishments as they see fit (Gil, 1970). Both preschoolers and teenagers are known for their difficult stages of development. Frustration in parents is often generated from young children going through the "terrible twos" stage and from teenagers going through a stage of rebellion and independence. Preschool children are too young to be reasoned with, and teenagers do not wish to be reasoned with. It is this ability to generate frustration within their parents and create stress in the family unit as a whole that places young children and teenagers in the vulnerable position of being victimized. Adolescents have reached a point in their development in being able to make effective use of the verbal skills they have acquired through years of conflict resolutions with family members. The biggest complaint among parents of adolescents in Steinmetz's study on parent-child conflict was the "smart talk mouthiness" used by adolescents in both sibling and parent-child interactions. Steinmetz describes the adolescents in her sample as being "verbally aggressive" and frequently engaging in hollering, threatening, and arguing (Steinmetz, 1977).

If the position of young children and teenagers is so similar in our society, why has society become so deeply concerned with protecting the rights of younger children while ignoring the plight of adolescents? The answer to this question can again be traced to differences in expectations parents have for their younger children versus their older children. Parents expect their adolescents to begin acting in a more mature and responsible manner as they approach adulthood. They expect adolescents to be able to follow orders and to begin internalizing their system of values. Parents do not hold the same expectations for their preschoolers. Therefore, when adolescents fail to live up to their parents' expectations of them, parents sometimes use physical force as a way of asserting their parental control. Society is more likely to condone the use of physical force directed at an adolescent due to the belief that adolescents deserve such treatment.

Adolescents are also perceived as being better able to fend for themselves in disputes with their parents. Adolescents are larger, stronger, and, therefore, better able to protect themselves or avoid confrontations altogether. While this may be true, Mulligan (1977), in her sample of over 250 college students attending an eastern university, found that 8 in 100 students in her sample had been physically injured by a parent while they lived at home during their senior year of high school. Even though children between the ages of five and fourteen are abused more frequently, children between the ages of fifteen and seventeen are more likely to have parents use "dangerous" forms of violence against them (Straus et al., 1980). In this case, examination of simple frequency statistics fails to tell the entire story regarding the seriousness of teenage victimization.

Extent of Violence Toward Adolescents

Although researchers are not in total agreement as to the exact extent of adolescent abuse, they do agree that violence toward adolescents is a legitimate and significant form of family violence that occurs more frequently than is generally assumed. In fact, researchers have been generally surprised at the rate at which parents were physically abusing their adolescent and teenage children. Data from Straus and his colleagues' nationally representative study on family violence (1980) reveal that 54 percent of preteen and early teenage children (ten to fourteen years of age) were struck by a parent while 33 percent of teens aged fifteen to seventeen were also hit during a one-year period (see Table 5.1). While younger children were more likely to be punched, grabbed, slapped, spanked, kicked, bitten, and hit with a fist or an object, teenage children were more likely to be "beat up" and have a knife or gun used against them. Very young children (under five) and teenagers were *the most likely to experience violence* that held a high chance of inflicting physical injury. Adolescents stand a good chance of being physically injured, regardless of their increased size and physical strength. Mulligan (1977) found that 30 percent of the college students she sampled who were attending an eastern university were victimized by a parent at least once during their senior year of high school. Also, 8 percent of these teenagers were physically injured. The acts of violence against teenagers go beyond the "normal" forms of aggression used to discipline children.

Sex and Age and Violence Toward Adolescents

Research findings depicting the relationship between sex and age of adolescents and the likelihood of violence and abuse are not always consistent. David Gil (1970), in his nationwide survey of child abuse, gathered information on abuse victims from cases reported through the central abuse registries in each state. He concluded that as children grow older, girls are more likely to be abused than boys. He attributed this finding to cultural attitudes regarding child-rearing practices in the United States. When children are younger, girls are more conforming than boys and require less discipline in the form of physical punishment. However, as children mature sexually, parents become more anxious over their daughters' heterosexual relationships. This anxiety leads to greater restrictions, increased conflict, and more frequent use of punishment to ensure parental control. With respect to boys, as they grow older, their physical strength increases and parents are less likely to use physical force for fear of retaliation. Also, the same anxieties that exist concerning the sexual activities of daughters do not exist for sons.

Other researchers have found the relationship between sex and age of adolescents and likelihood of abuse to be the exact opposite as that found by Gil (Mulligan, 1977; Straus et al., 1980). They found that young boys and girls were pushed, grabbed, shoved, slapped, and spanked at pretty much the same rate. But, as they grew older, boys over the age of ten were more likely to experience these forms of behavior than girls. Boys fifteen to seventeen were twice as likely as girls to be pushed, grabbed, or shoved. Mulligan (1977) reports that the higher rates of violence toward boys can be partially explained in terms of "linkage theory" (Straus, 1971), which states that parents socialize their children in accordance with the type of personality skills they feel their children will need later in life. If parents anticipate that their sons will be faced with aggressive situations more often than their daughters, parents will be more likely to use physical force toward their sons.

How can we explain the differences in the research findings concerning the age and sex of adolescents and their likelihood of abuse? Perhaps the answer lies in the techniques used by the researchers in collecting their information on abuse. Gil relied upon child abuse cases reported to public officials in the fifty states. Straus, Gelles, Steinmetz, and Mulligan relied upon self-reports of abuse. As has already been discussed in this book, the utilization of publicly identified cases of abuse has inherent problems. Perhaps girls were overrepresented in Gil's study because cases of abuse involving females were more likely to be reported to public officials than cases involving boys. The difference in findings may also be due to differences in the definition of abuse. Straus, Gelles, Steinmetz, and Mulligan focused on violence without concern for whether an injury took place. Gil's definition of abuse was restricted to cases that produced an injury. Gil also studied many more forms of abusive violence (e.g. burning) than Straus and his colleagues or Mulligan. Perhaps, females were more likely to be victims of the types of abuse not included in Straus and his colleagues' definition of victimization (such as strangling, drowning, burning, poisoning, or tying up or locking in).

Why are parents violent toward their adolescents and teenage children? One explanation is that they are violent and abusive toward their older children for the same reasons they are violent and abusive toward their younger children. Researchers however have not looked specifically at the causal factors associated with adolescent abuse. One possible factor might be the struggle for independence between adolescents and their parents. Adolescence is also a stressful period for children and parents. Another possible explanation is that parents see in their adolescent offspring the consequences of their parenting and may feel upset or guilty about their parent roles. Obviously, we need much more research on this issue in order to draw any kind of informed conclusion.

PARENT ABUSE

The idea of children attacking their parents is so foreign to our conceptions of parent-child relations that it is difficult for most of us to believe that such behavior occurs. Parents are granted the position of authority and power in the family's status hierarchy. Parents command control of the family's resources, such as money, power, status, and violence. According to the sociologist William Goode, violence *is* a legitimate resource at the disposal of family members, and it will be used whenever other attempts at alleviating a conflict fail. It is logically assumed, however, that the use of violence to resolve conflicts is brought into play by the typically dominant member of the family to ensure submission of those in their care. Goode argues that wives and children could, and sometimes do, use force but it does not occur frequently due to greater normative disapproval of children and wives using force against the father or husband.

> The rebellious child or wife knows the father or husband is stronger, and can call upon outsiders who will support that force with more force. . . . The force or threat they command is not only their own strength but that of the community, which will back up the traditional family patterns [Goode, 1971: 625-626].

The societal attitudes concerning who uses violence within the family partially explains why this form of violence is the least researched and consequently why not very much is known about its extent, patterns, and causes.

Goode's quote alludes to other social attitudes that hinder recognition of parent abuse as a hidden form of family violence. Not only do children lack control of the family's resources, but they are thought of as smaller and having less physical strength.

This observation alone is enough to make us think that children are not physically capable of injuring their parents. However, what research is available graphically demonstrates that children can and do inflict injury upon their parents. For example, one clinical study reports on the case of an eleven-year-old boy who became aggressive toward his mother after she spanked him for disobeying orders. He reportedly pushed her down, broke her coccyx, and then proceeded to kick her in the face while she was on the floor (Harbin and Madden, 1979: 1280). Carol Warren, (1978) in her investigation of fifteen battering adolescents between the ages of twelve and seventeen who were admitted to a psychiatric hospital, found that what these children lacked in physical strength, they more than made up for with speed and weapons. One twelve-year-old "poured gasoline in the bathroom while his mother was in there, threw a match, and shut the door." These examples demonstrate that physical size and strength are not always the best indicator as to who will be violent in a family.

Goode (1971) also quite accurately states that there is greater normative disapproval of children using violence against a parent than of a parent using violence against their children. The community supports parental rights and obligations while imposing strong sanctions against children who violate traditional family patterns concerning the legitimate use of force. Children abusing their parents is so counter-normative that it is extremely difficult for parents to admit that they are being victimized by one of their children. Unless the children commit lethal acts or acts of extreme violence, it is rare that the behavior of violent children and adolescents comes to the public's attention. Discussion and reporting of such acts is almost a taboo subject because many parents are ashamed of their own victimization. Parents are afraid that others will blame them for their children's violent behavior. Parents of abusive children are believed to suffer from tremendous anxiety, depression, and guilt. Henry Harbin and Dennis Madden (1979) examined fifteen families identified as having an adolescent between the ages of fourteen and twenty who was assaulting a parent. All these families were trying desperately to maintain an illusion of family harmony. Parents would occasionally admit to being abused by their children immediately following a particularly aggressive episode, but the "veil of denial" would rapidly reappear. Parents would try endlessly to protect their abusive offspring. Harbin and Madden identified four ways in which the veil of denial and protection manifested itself: (1) the families would try to avoid all discussion of the violent episodes; (2) all the family members would attempt to minimize the seriousness of the aggressive behavior; (3) the parents would avoid punishment for the abusive behavior; and (4) the families refused to ask for outside help for either themselves or for their child. The role of denial and the creation of an image of a peaceful and loving family plays an important part in abusive families. This role allows the family to continue functioning even though the family must continually deny the reality of violence (Ferreira, 1963). Admission of violent behavior on the part of the offspring or the parent may introduce the threat of family separation. The denial of reality serves as a defense mechanism to protect the family from outside observers and influence.

Extent of Violence Toward Parents

The few investigations of violence toward parents that have been conducted all report the same result: The rate of child-to-parent violence, while being less than parent-to-child abuse, is large enough to warrant attention. Most researchers agree that the rates at which children abuse their parents is around 10 percent. Martha Mulligan (1977) reports that 12 percent of the college students she questioned used at least one form of violence against a parent while they lived at home during their senior year of high school. Straus, Gelles, and Steinmetz (1980) found that 10 percent of the children three to seventeen years of age in their sample performed at least one act of violence against a parent during a one-year period (see Table 5.1). Our own statistics (Cornell and Gelles, 1982), generated from a nationally representative sample of families who had a teenager living at home between the ages of ten and seventeen, agreed with the findings of the other studies—9 percent of parents reported at least one act of violence. This translates into approximately 2.5 million parents being struck at least once a year. A statistic was also calculated for the more severe forms of violence. Approximately 3 percent of the adolescents were reported to have kicked, punched, bit, "beat-up," or used a knife or gun against a parent. While this percentage appears quite small, when it is projected to the total number of adolescents between ten and seventeen living in two parent households, it means that 900,000 parents are being abused each year.

Factors Related to Violence Toward Parents

Who is violent? Harbin and Madden (1979) found that the majority of children who attack a parent are between the ages of thirteen and twenty-four, although they also report on children as young as ten years old inflicting injury on their parents. Researchers agree that sons are slightly more likely to be violent and abusive than daughters. The sons' rates of severe violence against a parent increase with age, while for daughters the rates of severe violence decline with age. This suggests, perhaps, that boys do take advantage of increased size and strength that comes with adolescent growth. A social explanation could be that the boys and girls are adhering to the cultural norms that reward aggressiveness in teenage boys but negatively sanction the use of violence among teenage girls.

Most researchers support the belief that mothers are more likely to be abused than fathers. The typical situation of adolescent-to-parent violence appears to be older sons striking and abusing their mothers. It has been suggested that mothers may be the primary targets of violence and abuse for two reasons. First, mothers may lack the physical strength and/or social resources to effectively retaliate against their abusive children; and, second, children may learn that their mothers are an acceptable target for their violence. The data appear to suggest that children are more likely to abuse their mothers in homes where the mother is also a victim of spouse abuse.

Clinical observations of adolescents who had abused a parent found that most families had some disturbance in the authority structure within the family. Adolescents had been granted too much control. Abused parents seemed to be turning to young or immature children for decision making. This tremendous responsibility on the shoulders of young people seemed to generate extreme frustration. Harbin and Madden (1979) claim that the physical attacks on the parent were often an attempt by the adolescents to either control the family or to punish the parents for placing them in the decision-making role in the first place. Many of the abusive children had very poor self-concepts; whenever they were challenged or made to feel insecure, anxiety was created, often resulting in violent episodes.

While child abuse and spouse abuse have been found to be related to many social, family structural, and situational factors, adolescent violence does not seem to vary in any meaningful way with these same factors. Adolescent violence cannot be explained using the same social factors that explain adult violence. The data do appear to indicate, though, that the rates of parent abuse are related to the frequency of other forms of family violence within the home. The more violence children experience or witness, the more likely they are to strike out at a parent. These findings are consistent with the theory that families who view violence as a legitimate way to resolve conflict, run a greater risk of experiencing all forms of family violence, including parent abuse.

ELDER ABUSE

Abuse of the elderly is the only form of "hidden" family violence that has managed to generate a significant amount of public concern. This concern is, however, a very recent development. Prior to the 1980s, elder abuse received about as much social recognition as parent abuse, adolescent abuse, and sibling violence. There are several easily identifiable factors that can help explain society's recent interest in this topic. Major demographic changes, which have occurred over the last half century, have increased the number of older Americans in our population. This is a direct result of the life expectancy of the average person increasing by nearly 50 percent in approximately fifty years (U.S. Bureau of the Census, 1978). As elderly people live longer and the fertility rate declines, the proportion of elderly people in the population also increases. This growing number of older Americans has heightened our awareness of the many problems being experienced by the elderly. These changes have, in turn, had an impact upon family responsibilities. As people live longer, there is a growing need for middle-aged children to share the responsibility of caring for an aged parent. Of those between sixty-five and seventy-two years of age, only one elderly person in fifty needs long-term care. But, among those seventy-three years of age and over, the changes increase to one in fifteen (Koch and Koch, 1980). Children having the responsibility of caring for their aging parents is also a relatively new and growing aspect of family life. For these reasons, researchers have become interested in studying the consequences of caring for aging parents in the home. They realize that it is impractical to expect all families to have the appropriate financial, emotional, and social resources to handle this additional burden.

The recognition of elder abuse as a social problem and the subsequent identification of abuse victims has not been an easy task. Many obstacles have stood in the way. To begin with, the elderly are not tied into many social networks, such as mandatory schooling or employment, which facilitates easier identification of victims. The elderly are, on average, even more isolated from the mainstream of society than younger adults. This isolation allows violent behavior to continue unimpeded, with elderly victims confined to their homes, often dependent upon those who are abusing them. Identification of abuse victims is also hindered by the elderly victims' unwillingness to report incidents of maltreatment to the authorities. Only one in four known cases of abuse are reported by the victims themselves (Legal Research and Services for the Elderly, 1979). No one knows how many cases exist that go unreported! Sometimes friends, relatives, or neighbors are aware of what is happening but they are frightened and unsure of what to do. In the majority of cases, however, elder abuse becomes known to the authorities through a third party (Legal Research and Services for the Elderly, 1979). Even after the occurrence of abuse has been reported and substantiated, many abuse victims are unwilling to admit to it.

There are a number of reasons to explain their hesitancy. Due to societal attitudes, many elderly family members are too embarrassed to admit that they have raised a child capable of such behavior. Again, as with other forms of family violence, they assume the blame for their abuser's behavior. Frequently, their love for their abuser is stronger than the desire to leave the abusive situation. They are more concerned for the welfare of their abuser than for their own safety and well-being. They are unwilling to begin any legal action that might result in some sort of punishment for their abuser and consequently, further their own isolation. This fear of isolation is a result of the majority of victims living in the same house as their abuser (Legal Research and Services for the Elderly, 1979). If elderly people are physically, emotionally, or economically dependent upon their abusers, they may be unsure of what alternatives are available to them if they do report the abuse. An important problem is that the alternatives available to aged family members who may wish to leave an abusive environment are often considered worse than the abusive situation. In particular, the elderly victim often considers institutionalized care as the worst possible alternative. This fear of institutionalization is apparently a valid one. Lau and Kosberg (1979), in their study of abuse victims reported to the Cleveland Chronic Illness Center, report that 46 percent of the cases of elder abuse eventually resulted in institutionalization of the victim. In 26 percent of the cases, assistance was refused by the victim and in 28 percent of the cases assistance other than institutionalization was offered and accepted.

Another factor that hinders identification of abuse victims is the low level of awareness among public service agencies regarding the issue of elderly abuse. Agencies dealing with the elderly were initially very reluctant to become involved in abuse cases. They were concerned about violations of confidentiality. When the issue of confidentiality had been resolved, the agencies often did not have available the personnel and resources to effectively handle reported cases. It has been noted that these were precisely the same issues that hindered action in the identification, awareness, and treatment of child abuse twenty years earlier (Rathbone-McCuan, 1980).

Nature and Extent of Elder Abuse

Abusive treatment toward the elderly can take on many forms. Caretakers may tie an aged relative to a bed or chair while they go out shopping or finish their housework. They may over-medicate their parents to "ease" the older person's discomfort and to make them more manageable. Other caretakers resort to physical attacks to "make them mind" or to coerce their elderly relatives into changing a will or signing the house or social security checks over to them. Some caretakers have used such excessive physical violence or have neglected the needs of the older person to such an extent that death has resulted.

It is difficult to assess exactly how many elderly people are abused each year. While several state agencies have tried to assess the extent of abuse in their individual states, resources have not been allocated to conduct a nationally representative study. The frequency of elder abuse could vary from 500,000 cases a year (for only acts of physical violence) to 2.5 million cases annually (U.S. Congress, 1980). The larger estimates of elder abuse have resulted from defining "abuse" as physical, emotional, psychological, and self-abuse, in addition to passive and active neglect. The development of an adequate and acceptable definition of elder abuse has been, perhaps, the most significant impediment in developing an adequate knowledge base on elder abuse. The variety of definitions in the current studies makes the task of comparing the results of the research nearly impossible. Naturally, the broader one's definition of abuse, the greater the number of incidents per year.

Based upon the existing data, the most likely victim of elder abuse is a female of very advanced age. The victims usually suffer from physical and/or mental impairments and are dependent upon their caretakers for many, if not most, of their daily needs (Block and Sinnott, 1979; Legal Research and Services for the Elderly, 1979; Rathbone-McCuan, 1980; Steinmetz, 1978c). It is this dependent situation of the elderly that increases their likelihood of being abused. Suzanne Steinmetz (1978c) notes that several parallels exist between child abuse and elderly abuse. Both children and the elderly are in dependent positions in the family and rely upon their caregivers for the provision of basic needs. Both are presumed to be protected and adequately cared for within the family setting, and both can become a source of economic, physical, or emotional strain. Steinmetz believes that while most couples expect to care for children, they do not always anticipate the possibility of caring for their aged parents. The process of caring for elderly parents presents unique problems for any family. While children become less and less dependent with age, the health of aging relatives renders them more and more dependent.

Factors Related to Elder Abuse

The abuser is typically identified as being female, middle-aged, and usually the offspring of the abused. Often middle-aged couples begin caring for an elderly parent at the time when their own children are beginning to leave home. Placing the couple back into a nurturing role, just when they expected to be completing this responsibility, creates stress for the caretaker. The caretaker, usually a woman, must again defer her personal goals and cater to the needs of a dependent person. If families provide a home for an aging relative while the children are still living at home, the family resources must be reallocated to include another dependent member. This can create stress in mothers who are already trying to meet the demands of their children and spouse and now must care for another person.

Stress is almost always identified as a contributing factor to elder abuse. It is unrealistic to expect all families to be able to assume the responsibility of caring for an aging parent, just as it was unrealistic to expect all people raising children to do so successfully. Families may lack the appropriate levels of personal, social, and economic resources to adequately nurture their dependent, aging relatives.

Researchers find that many victims of elder abuse were at one time abusive toward their children. Elder abuse may sometimes simply be an extension of the child abuse syndrome. The adult children learned, through personal experience or observation, that the use of violence was an acceptable response to a stressful situation. The violent resolution of stressful situations runs in the family and is passed on from generation to generation.

SUMMARY

It is quite clear that the rates of the "hidden" forms of private violence are as high or higher than the better-known types of violence. Our understanding of the hidden victims of violence is limited because there has been very little research on these forms of violence. The data on sibling violence and violence toward parents are either anecdotal or come from Straus and his colleagues' National Family Violence Survey (1980). Even in that survey, sibling violence and violence toward parents was added as almost an afterthought, and the survey failed to ask many questions specific to these types of violence. Data on elder abuse are limited, and when available, come from small samples or case studies. Similarly, data on violence toward adolescents come either from small case studies, or come from parts of the National Family Violence Survey.

One hopes that as we gain a better understanding of violence in the home, we will recognize that it is certainly not directed solely toward young children and women. A perspective that recognizes that all family relationships can be and sometimes are violent might help us to broaden our examination into the generative sources of intimate violence. The next chapter attempts to apply that broader perspective and pose a general theory of family violence.

DISCUSSION QUESTIONS

1. Why have the "hidden forms" of family violence been overlooked? How does blaming the victim contribute to keeping certain forms of family violence hidden? How do cultural norms and values concerning children, parents, and the elderly contribute to keeping certain forms of family violence hidden?

2. Why has elderly abuse received more attention than the other forms of hidden violence?

3. What are some of the factors related to hidden forms of violence? How do the factors related to hidden violence compare to factors related to the abuse of young children or violence between spouses?

SUGGESTED ASSIGNMENTS

1. Find out if your state has mandatory reporting laws for cases of elder abuse. Who is required to report? How many cases are reported each year? Has there been an increase in reporting in the last few years? What services are available in your community, city, or state for victims of elder abuse?

2. Conduct a survey and measure people's awareness of and attitudes toward the known forms of family violence (child abuse or wife abuse) and the hidden forms. Be sure to ask parallel questions so that you can compare the results.

CHAPTER
6

Explaining
Family Violence

THE DISCUSSION IN PREVIOUS CHAPTERS about the factors that are
related to various types of family violence shed some light on our
understanding of why parents batter children, husbands abuse
wives, and other family members assault their siblings and parents. Nevertheless, a list of factors associated with family violence still does not complete our understanding. People with low
incomes may be more likely to abuse a family member, but
income is *not a complete explanation* of family violence.

This chapter first examines profiles of child and wife batterers
in order to get a composite picture of how the various factors
combine to produce violence. The following section poses the
question, Why is the family such a violent institution? The answer
can be found by looking at some of the unique characteristics of
the family as a social group. Finally, we review some of the
models that have been used to explain family violence, and we
conclude with an integrated social exchange/social control
explanation.

PROFILES OF VIOLENT HOMES

One way of advancing our understanding of family violence is
to move beyond a simple examination of single factors and their
association with violence. After considering all the variables that
are found to be related with violence in the home, Straus and his
colleagues added the factors together to get a profile of child
abusers and spouse abusers.

A Profile of Child Abuse

Although it is really impossible to characterize the "typical"
child abuser, there are a number of characteristics of individuals
and families which, when combined, increase the chances that
abuse will occur.

Homes with the greatest risk of child abuse are homes characterized by Straus and associates (1980) by

1. both parents being verbally aggressive to the children;
2. more than the average amount of conflict between the husband and wife;
3. the husband being verbally aggressive toward his wife;
4. the husband being aggressive toward his wife;
5. the husband being a manual worker;
6. the husband being dissatisfied with his standard of living;
7. the wife being a manual worker or a full-time housekeeper;
8. the wife being less than thirty years old;
9. the wife and the husband having been physically punished as children;
10. two or more children in the home;
11. the couple having been married less that ten years;
12. having lived in neighborhood fewer than two years;
13. the father participating in no organized community groups; or
14. the father growing up in a family where his mother hit his father.

Families that failed to include any one of the above characteristics reported *no* abusive violence toward children. Families where all fourteen factors were present had a three in ten chance of using abusive violence toward their children. Obviously, this is not a perfect explanation for the presence or absence of child abuse, but it does give some insight into what kinds of situations increase the risk of abuse for children.

A Profile of Wife Abuse

Straus and associates found twenty characteristics relevant in acts of wife beating. They included:

1. the husband employed part-time or unemployed;
2. family income under $6000;
3. the husband a manual worker (if employed);

4. both husband and wife very worried about economic security;
5. the wife dissatisfied with the family's standard of living;
6. two or more children;
7. disagreements over children being common;
8. husband and wife having grown up in families where the father hit the mother;
9. couples married fewer than ten years;
10. the husband and wife both less than thirty years of age;
11. a nonwhite racial group;
12. above average marital conflict;
13. very high levels of family and individual stress;
14. the wife or husband dominating family decisions;
15. a husband verbally aggressive to his wife;
16. a wife verbally aggressive to her husband;
17. both getting drunk frequently, but are not alcoholics;
18. couples who lived in a neighborhood fewer than two years;
19. couples who do not participate in organized religion; or
20. the wife a full-time housewife.

Again, as with the profile of child abusive families, if none of these characteristics was present, there was no reported spouse abuse in the home. Those families that were unfortunate enough to have more than twelve of the factors had better than a six in ten chance of some reported wife abuse in the previous year.

It might be tempting to think that we could use these profiles to predict where and when family abuse will occur. Unfortunately, this would generate many more problems than it would solve. Since the profiles are not 100 percent accurate (for example, 70 percent of the homes with all the child abuse risk factors still do not abuse their children; three in ten families with all the wife abuse characteristics do not have wife abuse), we would run the very dangerous risk of falsely predicting many people as child or wife beaters. The negative consequences of false labeling would certainly cancel out the good that would be derived from being able to predict, in advance, some families who will become abusive.

VIOLENCE AND
THE ORGANIZATION OF FAMILY LIFE

For much of this book we have concentrated on examining the characteristics of individuals and family relations and how these characteristics are related to various types of family violence. To concentrate only on individuals and family relations would, to a certain extent, miss the forest for the trees. While many people consider the most important questions in the study of family violence to be, "Who are the abusive family members and why are they abusive?" another equally important question is, "Why are families so violent?" Once we have completed our examination of the incidence and extent of the various types of family violence, we are left with the quite inescapable conclusion that the family is society's most violent institution, excepting only the military in times of war. Why is the family the place where you are the most likely to be killed, physically assaulted, hit, beat up, slapped, or spanked? Why is violence perhaps as common as love in families? Until we consider the social organization of the family that makes it violence prone, we have not adequately addressed the questions we opened this book with.

Murray Straus and Richard Gelles (1979) identified the unique characteristics of the family as a social group that contribute to making the family a violent-prone institution. Later, Straus, with his colleague Gerald Hotaling (1979), noted the irony that these same characteristics we saw as making the family violent-prone also serve to make the family a warm, supportive, and intimate environment. Briefly, these factors are:

1. *Time at Risk.* The ratio of time spent interacting with family members far exceeds the ratio of time spent interacting with others, although the ratio will vary depending on stages in the family life cycle.
2. *Range of Activities and Interests.* Not only do family members spend a great deal of time with one another, the interaction

ranges over a much wider spectrum of activities than nonfamilial interaction.

3. *Intensity of Involvement.* The quality of family interaction is also unique. The degree of commitment to family interaction is greater. A cutting remark made by a family member is likely to have a much larger impact than the same remark in another setting.

4. *Impinging Activities.* Many interactions in the family are inherently conflict-structured and have a "zero sum" aspect. Whether it involves deciding what television show to watch or what car to buy, there will be both winners and losers in family relations.

5. *Right to Influence.* Belonging to a family carries with it the implicit right to influence the values, attitudes, and behaviors of other family members.

6. *Age and Sex Differences.* The family is unique in that it is made up of different ages and sexes. Thus, there is the potential for a battle between generations *and* sexes.

7. *Ascribed Roles.* In addition to the problem of age and sex differences is the fact that the family is perhaps the only social institution that assigns roles and responsibilities based on age and sex rather than interest or competence.

8. *Privacy.* The modern family is a private institution, insulated from the eyes, ears, and often rules of the wider society. Where privacy is high, the degree of social control will be low.

9. *Involuntary Membership.* Families are exclusive organizations. Birth relationships are involuntary and cannot be terminated. While there can be ex-wives and ex-husbands, there are no ex-children or ex-parents. Being in a family involves personal, social, material, and legal commitment and entrapment. When conflict arises it is not easy to break off the conflict by fleeing the scene or resigning from the group.

10. *Stress.* Families are prone to stress. This is due in part to the theoretical notion that dyadic relationships are unstable (Simmel, 1950). Moreover, families are constantly undergoing changes and transitions. The birth of children, maturation of children, aging, retirement, and death are all changes recognized by family scholars. Moreover, stress felt by one family member (such as unemployment, illness, bad grades at school) is transmitted to other family members.

11. *Extensive Knowledge of Social Biographies.* The intimacy and emotional involvement of family relations reveals a full range of

identities to members of a family. Strengths and vulnerabilities, likes and dislikes, loves and fears are all known to family members. While this knowledge can help support a relationship, the information can also be used to attack intimates and lead to conflict.

It is one thing to say that the social organization of the family makes it a conflict-prone institution and social group. However, the eleven characteristics we listed do not supply the total answer. The key additional consideration is one we discussed in Chapter 2. The fact that the social organization of the family we have just described exists within a cultural context where violence is tolerated, accepted, and even mandated is a critical factor which helps us understand why the family, as currently structured, can be loving, supportive, *and* violent. The widespread acceptability of physical punishment to raise children creates a situation where a conflict-prone institution serves as a training ground to teach children that it is acceptable (1) to hit people you love, (2) for powerful people to hit less powerful people, (3) to use hitting to achieve some end or goal, and (4) to hit as an end in itself.

MODELS THAT EXPLAIN FAMILY VIOLENCE

The Psychiatric Model

Although we have discussed the psychiatric model previously and have found that this explanation for family violence is too limited, its popularity in the professional literature as well as among the general public causes us to repeat the model and its problems one more time.

The tragic picture of a defenseless child, woman, or grandparent subjected to abuse and neglect arouses the strongest emotions in clinicians and others who see and/or treat the problem of intimate violence. There frequently seems to be no rational explanation for harming a loved one. It is not surprising, therefore, that a psychiatric model of family violence was the first applied to the problem and has endured for years, even in the absence of strong scientific evidence to support such a model. Even sociologists can find themselves using such a model. One of us (Gelles) once was working in a clinic at Children's Hospital of Boston. We were examining and doing a psycho-social-medical evaluation of a young child who had suffered a severe immersion burn (she had been forced into a bathtub filled with scalding hot water). It was obvious that she had been purposely burned, since she had been pressed against the tub with such force that neither the soles of her feet or her bottom had been burned. After the scalding, she had apparently been tied to the bed and this had resulted in lacerations of her wrists and ankles. After our examination, we returned to our offices and wrote up our clinic notes. Our colleague, Eli Newberger (he is referenced at times in this text), came by and asked us what we thought of the case. We responded, "Anyone who would do that is crazy!" Eli looked puzzled. "Aren't you the person who wrote in 1973 that the psychopathological model of abuse was a myth?" he asked Gelles. (I did, and my model is presented in Chapter 3, RJG.) "I don't care what I wrote," Gelles responded, "I know what I saw!"

The psychiatric model focuses on the abuser's personality characteristics as the chief determinants of violence and abuse. A psychiatric model links factors such as mental illness, personality defects, psychopathology, sociopathology, alcohol and drug misuse, or other intra-individual abnormalities to family violence.

Research indicates that less than 10 percent of instances of family violence is attributable solely to personality traits, mental illness, or psychopathology (Steele, 1978).

In closing this discussion, it is important to speculate why, despite the lack of scientific evidence, people (including us, at times) persist in applying the psychiatric model to more cases of family violence than is warranted. The answer may lie, paradoxically, in the fact that family violence is so extensive in our society that we do not want to recognize it as a pattern of family relations. Somehow, we do not want to consider our own potential to abuse or even consider that some of the acts we engage in (pushing a wife, slapping a child) are violent or abusive. If we can persist in believing that violence and abuse are the products of aberrations or sickness, then if we believe ourselves to be well, then our acts cannot be hurtful or abusive. Furthermore, the psychiatric model serves as an ideal smokescreen to blind us from considering social organizational factors that cause family violence.

A Social-Situational Model

That personality problems and psychopathology do not fully explain acts of family·violence does not mean that personal problems are unrelated to intimate abuse. These personal problems, however, tend to arise from social antecedents. We have reviewed in previous chapters those social factors such as conflict, unemployment, isolation, unwanted pregnancy, and stress.

A social situational model of family violence proposes that abuse and violence arise out of two main factors. The first is structural stress. The association between low income and family violence, for instance, indicates that a central factor in violence and abuse is inadequate financial resources. The second main factor is the cultural norm concerning force and violence in the home (see Chapter 2).."Spare the rod and spoil the child." "The marriage license is a hitting license." These are phrases that underscore the widespread social approval for the use of force and violence at home.

The social-situational model notes that such structural stresses as low income, unemployment, limited educational resources, illness, and the like are unevenly distributed in society. While all groups are told that they should be loving parents, adoring husbands, and caring wives, only some groups get sufficient resources to meet these demands. Others fall considerably short of being able to have the psychological, social, and economic resources to meet the expectations of society, friends, neighbors, loved ones, and themsleves. Combined with the cultural approval for violence, these shortfalls lead many family members to adopt violence and abuse as a means of coping with structural stress.

Social Learning Theory

A subset of social-situational theory is social learning theory. A commonly stated explanation for family violence is that people learn to be violent when they grow up in violent homes. The family is the first place where people learn the roles of mother and father, husband and wife. The family is one key place where we learn how to cope with stress and frustration. The family is also the place where people are most likely to first experience violence. We have seen already in previous chapters that violence is frequently transmitted from generation to generation. Again, we must warn that not all violence victims grow up to be violent themselves. But, a history of abuse and violence does increase the risk that an individual will be violent as an adult.

Individuals are not only exposed to techniques of being violent, but they also learn the social and moral justifications for the behavior. It is not uncommon to hear a parent who has physically struck his or her own child explain that they were punishing the child for the child's own good. We have interviewed many parents who use exactly the same physical punishment on their children that they themselves experienced (some even use the exact same objects, which must be passed down from generation to generation).

Resource Theory

Another explanation of family violence that is supported by the available scientific data is resource theory (Goode, 1971). This model assumes that all social systems (including the family) rest to some degree on force or the threat of force. The more resources—social, personal, and economic—a person can command, the more force he or she can muster. However, according to William Goode, the author of this theory, the more resources a person actually has, the less he or she will actually use force in an open manner. Thus, a husband who wants to be the dominant person in the family, but has little education, has a job low in prestige and income, and lacks interpersonal skills, may choose to use violence to maintain the dominant position. In addition, family members (including children) may use violence to redress a grievance when they have few alternative resources available.

An Ecological Perspective

The psychologist James Garbarino (1977) has proposed an "ecological model" to explain the complex nature of child maltreatment. Garbarino applies what he refers to as the ecological or human development approach. This model concentrates on the progressive, mutual adaptation of the organism (in this case, family members) and the environment. Garbarino concerns himself not just with the family, but with the complex interrelation of the many social systems that overlap with family life and influence human development. A major concern of Garbarino's is "social habitability" or the quality of the environment in which the person and family develop. Garbarino also considers the political, economic, and social factors that shape the quality of life for children and their families.

From these complex series of overlapping factors and influences, Garbarino extracts two key elements that help explain the existence of child abuse. First, as has been so often stated, is the cultural support for using physical force against children. Second, is the level of family support in the environment. The less family support (one factor might be fewer available day care centers), the greater the risk of maltreatment of children.

In short, the ecological model proposes that violence and abuse arise out of a mismatch of parent to child and family to neighborhood and community. To somewhat oversimplify, the risk of abuse and violence is greatest when the functioning of the children and parents is limited and constrained by developmental problems. Children with learning disabilities, social or emotional handicaps are at increased risk for abuse. Parents under considerable stress or who have personality problems are at increased risk for abusing their children. These conditions are worsened when social interaction between the spouses or the parents and children heighten the stress or make the personal problems worse. Finally, if there are few institutions and agencies in the community to support troubled families, then the risk of abuse is further raised.

Garbarino has found that the highest rates of child abuse are found in communities that have the fewest human and social service agencies. Rates are high in homes where marital conflict and stress are the highest and among families who are socially isolated. Last, specific personal and social characteristics of children and parents increase the likelihood for abuse.

Patriarchy and Wife Abuse

The previous models of family violence have been different only in degrees. They tend to examine individuals and family relations in their search for the explanation for family violence. The final model we examine is quite different. The sociologists Russell and Rebecca Dobash (1979) see wife abuse as a unique phenomenon that has been obscured and overshadowed by what they refer to as the "narrow" focus on domestic violence. As we noted earlier in this book the Dobashes make the case that throughout history, violence has systematically been directed toward women. The Dobashes' central thesis is that economic and social processes operate directly and indirectly to support a patriarchal (male dominated) social order and family structure. Their central theoretical argument is that patriarchy leads to the subordination of women and causes the historical pattern of systematic violence directed against wives.

The Dobashes' theory is perhaps the only theory that finds the source of family violence in the society and how it is organized, as opposed to within individual families or communities. The major drawback of the theory is that it uses but a single factor (patriarchy) to explain violence, and single factor explanations are rarely useful in social science.

AN EXCHANGE/SOCIAL CONTROL THEORY OF FAMILY VIOLENCE

Some time ago we were called by a newspaper reporter who was writing an editorial on family violence. He wanted us to give him a short one- or two-sentence statement on why family members used violence on one another. At first, the thought of boiling down eleven years of research into some kind of quotable-quote seemed impossible. But we had been wrestling for some time with a project that was aimed at developing an integrated theory of family violence. We wanted a theory that was applicable to child abuse, wife abuse, and the hidden forms of intimate violence. One attempt to develop an integrated theory failed miserably when the resulting model was so complex that we had a hard time following it ourselves when we had to proofread the figure for a book in which it was to be published. While we wanted to borrow the best and most useful elements from the theories we reviewed, this seemed to be impossible.

As a consequence, we turned to trying to develop a more "middle range" (Merton, 1945) theory. Exchange or choice theory seemed to be a framework that best integrated the key elements of the diverse theories. Moreover, exchange theory also had the virtue of providing a suitable perspective to explain and answer a variety of questions and issues in the study of family violence, such as "Why do battered women remain with violent men?"

And so, we responded to the newspaper reporters by stating:

> "People hit and abuse family members because *they can*."

The reporter was quite taken aback. He wanted a simple statement, but this seemed too simple. To better understand what it implies, and why it is not simple at all, one has to know and appreciate some of the key assumptions of exchange theory.

Key Assumptions of Exchange Theory

An assumption of exchange theory that is relevant in explaining family violence is that human interaction is guided by the pursuit of rewards and the avoidance of punishment and costs. In addition, an individual who supplies reward services to another obliges him or her to fulfill an obligation, and thus the second individual must furnish benefits to the first (Blau, 1964). If reciprocal exchange of rewards occurs, the interaction will continue. But if reciprocity is not received, the interaction will be broken off.

Intrafamilial relations are more complex than those studied by traditional exchange theorists. In some instances it is not feasible or possible to break off interaction, even if there is not reciprocity. When the "principle of distributive justice" is violated, there can be increased anger, resentment, conflict, and violence.

Many students of family violence tend to view violence as the last resort to solving problems in the family. Nye (1979), however, notes that this need not be the case. Spanking, for instance, is frequently the first choice of action by many parents.

When we say that *people hit family members because they can*, we are applying the basic assumptions of exchange theory to the case of family violence. We expect that people will only use violence toward family members when the costs of being violent do not outweigh the rewards.

There are a variety of costs for being violent. First, there is the potential that the victim will hit back. Second, a violent assault could lead to the arrest and/or imprisonment of the person who has done the hitting. Using violence could also lead to a loss of status. Finally, too much violence might lead to the dissolution of the family. Thus, there are potential significant costs involved in being violent.

Social control is a means of raising the costs of violent behavior. Police intervention, criminal charges, imprisonment, loss of status, loss of income are all forms of social control that could raise the costs and lower the rewards of violent behavior.

From these basic assumptions, we find that there are certain structural properties of families that make them violent prone, and there are specific family and individual traits that make certain families more at risk for violence than other families.

Inequality, Privacy, Social Controls, and Violence

We can expand our first proposition that people hit family members because they can into three propositions:

1. Family members are more likely to use violence in the home when they expect the costs of being violent to be less than the rewards.
2. The absence of effective social controls (e.g. police intervention) over family relations decreases the costs of one family member being violent toward another.
3. Certain social and family structures reduce social control in family relations and, therefore, reduce the costs and increase the rewards of being violent.

Inequality in the home can both reduce the social control and reduce the costs of being violent. The *private nature* of the modern family serves to reduce the degree of social control exercised over family relations (Laslett, 1973; 1978). Finally, the *image of the "real man"* in society also reduces social control in the home and increases the rewards of being violent.

Inequality. The normative power structure in society and the family and the resulting sexual and generational inequality in the family serves to reduce the chances that victims of family violence can threaten or inflict harm on offenders. Husbands are typically bigger than wives, have higher status positions, and earn more money. Because of this, they can use violence without fear of being struck back hard enough to be injured. Moreover, they do not risk having their wives take economic or social sanctions against them. Parents can use violence toward their children without fear that their children can strike back and injure them. The fact that the use of violence toward children by mothers decreases with the child's age (Gelles and Hargreaves, 1981) can be interpreted as a consequence of the greater risk of being hit back as the child grows older and larger.

Women and children may be the most frequent victims of family violence because they have no place to run and are not strong enough or do not possess sufficient resources to inflict costs on their attackers.

Privacy. Victims of family violence could turn to outside agencies to redress their grievances, but the private nature of the family reduces the accessibility of outside agencies of social control. Neighbors who report that they overhear incidents of family violence also say that they fear intervening in another person's home. Police, prosecutors, and courts are reluctant to pursue cases involving domestic violence. When these cases are followed up, the courts are faced with the no-win position of either doing nothing or separating the combatants. Thus, to protect a child, judges may view as their only alternative to remove the child from the home. To protect the woman, the solution may be a separation or divorce. Either situation puts the legal system in the position of breaking up a family to protect the individual members. Because courts typically view this as a drastic step, such court-ordered separations or removals are comparatively rare, unless there is stark evidence of repeated grievous injury.

Violence and the "Real Man." One last cost of being violent is the loss of social status that goes along with being labeled a "child beater" or a "wife beater." However, there are subcultures where aggressive sexual and violent behavior is considered proof that someone is a "real man" (Toby, 1966). Thus, rather than risk status loss, the violent family members may actually realize a status gain. Moreover, that notion that "a man's home is his castle" reduces external social control over family life.

In situations where status can be lost by being violent, individuals employ accepted vocabularies of motive (Mills, 1940) or "accounts" (Lyman and Scott, 1970) to explain their behavior. Thus, a violent father or mother might explain their actions by saying they were drunk or lost control. Parents who shared the same desire to batter their children might nod in agreement without realizing that a real loss of control would have produced a much more grievous injury or even death.

Applying Exchange/Social Control Theory

An exchange/social control theory approach to family violence can be extremely helpful in explaining some of the patterns of family violence that have been uncovered in recent empirical investigations.

The child abuse literature notes that certain types of children are at greater risk for abuse. Ill, handicapped, premature, ugly, and demanding children are at greater risk of being abused by their parents. These children either make great demands on their parents (economically, socially, or psychologically), or, as in the case of deformed children or children seen as ugly by their parents, may be perceived as not providing sufficient gratification in return for the parents' investment of time and energy. In any case, when a parent perceives the costs of parenting to outweigh the rewards, the alternatives are limited. The relationship between parent and child is difficult to break—with the exception of giving the child up for adoption or foster care, or the death of the child or parent. Thus, with few alternatives and high dissatisfaction, the parent may resort to violence or abuse.

A similar combination of lack of alternatives and imbalance of effort invested and rewards received may be helpful in understanding other violent family relationships. Also, it is important not to lose sight of the fact that violence itself may be rewarding. Exchange theorists note that to inflict "costs" on someone who has injured you may be rewarding. The idea of "revenge being sweet" can be used to explain why wives resort to severe forms of violence in response to being punched or hit by their husbands. Also, children who assault parents who were violent, and middle-aged women who assault their elderly mothers (who may have been violent when younger), are examples of this principle of exchange theory.

The sociologist F. Ivan Nye (1979) has applied exchange theory to family violence and developed a number of theoretical propositions. First, he stated:

> Violence in the family is more frequent in societies that have no legal or other normative structure prohibiting it. In societies that prohibit violence against some members (wives) but permit it against others (children), violence will be less frequent toward those members against whom it is prohibited than toward those against whom it is allowed.

Nye goes on to propose that wife beating and child beating are less common in families that have relatives and/or friends nearby, while child beating is more common in single-parent than in two-parent families. We would recast his propositions to read:

> Family violence is more common when non-nuclear family members (e.g., friends, relatives, bystanders) are unavailable, unable, or unwilling to be part of the daily system of family interaction, and thus unable to serve as agents of formal and informal social control.

In terms of the general pattern of relationships among family members, the greater the disparity between perceived investment in a family relationship such as parenting, and the perceived returns on the investment, the greater the likelihood that there will be violence. The fact that children three to five years of age and children fifteen to seventeen years of age were found to be the most likely victims of child abuse could be the result of parents of younger children perceiving a rather large investment in their children while getting little in the way of actual return. Parents who abuse teenage children (and risk being hit back) may do so because they may believe that their investment in rearing the children has yielded disappointing results.

These propositions again tend to view violence as a last resort or final alternative to an imbalance of investment and rewards in family relations. It is important to note that violence could be the first resort. Spanking children may be common because it is culturally approved and because it is immediately gratifying to the parent. Many parents justify their use of violence as a child rearing technique because it tends to bring with it immediate emotional reward for the parent and immediate cessation of the child's offending or perceived offending behavior.

Exchange theory is also useful for explaining other findings in the study of family violence. The fact that pregnant women are at risk of physical abuse by their husbands may be partly due to the helplessness of these women and their inability to hit back. Parents who overestimate their children's ability and capabilities may abuse them because these parents expect more out of the relationship with the children than they receive.

TOWARD PREVENTING AND TREATING FAMILY VIOLENCE

One of the virtues of an exchange/social control theory of family violence is that it has direct applications to the prevention and treatment of intimate violence. Again, to oversimplify, if violence occurs in families because family members *can* be violent, then the goal of prevention and treatment is to make it so they cannot. To do this requires practitioners and social policy planners to consider how they can increase the degree of social control over families, raise the costs of violence, and reduce the rewards. The final chapter of this text considers programs and policies that are designed to treat violent families as well as preventing violence before it can occur.

DISCUSSION QUESTIONS

1. Why would it be improper and perhaps even harmful to use the profiles of violent families presented in this chapter to predict which families will abuse children or spouses?

2. How does the private nature of the family contribute to both love and violence within families?

3. What are some of the "rewards" of being violent in families?

SUGGESTED ASSIGNMENTS

1. Design model legislation for either child abuse or wife abuse that would raise the costs of violence in families.

2. Assume that you have been asked to testify before a state legislature or Congress on the topic of preventing family violence. Based on the theories that attempt to explain family violence, what would you recommend? Prepare your testimony.

CHAPTER 7

Prevention and Treatment

Society's Response and Responsibility

IF PEOPLE ARE VIOLENT toward family members because they can be violent, because the advantages of violence outweigh the costs, because the privacy of the family and social attitudes decrease social control, then how do we break the cycle of violence? How do we protect victims of violence? More important, how can we prevent violence from occurring? We concluded the previous chapter by stating that the goal of prevention and treatment is to make it so people can't be violent. But what does this mean? What programs and policies will make it so people can't be violent? What should we do?

Initially, the response to family violence was to assume that abusive family members were mentally ill. But over the past two decades the tendency to diagnose the causes of violence as a psychological abnormality or mental illness has declined. We realize now that individual psychiatric care for violent family members is but one limited treatment for the problem. Since the roots of family violence lie in the structure of the family and society, we know that individual psychiatric treatment can be effective with only a small number of cases of violence and abuse. Individual and family counseling are still important steps in intervening in family violence, but a variety of programs and policies have been developed that deal with other structural sources of violence. We begin this chapter by reviewing the steps that have been taken to aid in discovering private violence. Over the past two decades, laws have been passed and policies have been implemented by the criminal justice system to help recognize and identify various forms of family violence. But recognition and identification of violence and abuse are but the first step in treating and preventing violence in the home. Intervention once an instance of violence is publicly identified poses an important problem. Should we respond with efforts to *control* violence in the home, or should our approach be one of *compassion*? We examine the dilemma of compassion versus control in the next section. The following section reviews the various treatment programs that have been developed to deal with various types of family violence. Finally, the chapter concludes with a discussion of prevention, and we present a number of important steps that should be taken if we want to reduce the tragic toll of family violence in society.

FROM BEHIND CLOSED DOORS: RECOGNIZING FAMILY VIOLENCE

Child Abuse: Reporting Laws

Because violence was hidden behind the closed doors of the American household for so many years, one of the initial policy approaches was to make sure that abuse and violence were recognized publically so that human service professionals could respond with the proper treatment. In the first decade after child abuse was recognized as a significant health and social problem, a great amount of effort went into assuring that abused children would be identified and responded to with the proper treatment. Between 1962 and 1970, all 50 states enacted mandatory child abuse reporting laws that required designated professionals to report suspected cases of child abuse. Mandatory reporting laws were designed to bring child abuse out from behind closed doors. There are many professionals who see children daily and who see the visible and emotional signs of abuse and neglect. However, prior to the enactment of reporting laws, many professionals, including physicians and teachers, were extremely reluctant to report cases of child abuse. The reasons for failing to report were many and varied. Some professionals were unaware of the signs of abuse and often accepted the explanation that the bruises and scars were the results of accidents. Even if the signs of abuse were clearly identifiable (for instance, a handmark on the side of the face), professionals were still reluctant to become involved in what most people considered to be a "family matter." Fear of being sued for false accusation also played a part in failure to report. Last, professionals and the public alike frequently did not know who to report cases of abuse to.

Gradually, state laws were drafted that mandated specific professionals (or in some states, all adults) to report suspected abuse. In order to protect people who made reports in good faith, state statutes provided that people making reports in good faith could not be sued for false accusation. When it appeared that the early versions of the law still were not generating adequate numbers of reports, some states added criminal penalties for failing to report cases of suspected abuse. In addition to passing laws, states also engaged in public awareness campaigns and public education programs. The initial impact of such campaigns was startling. Florida began one of the first public awareness programs in the early 1970s. Along with the program, Florida provided a toll-free number for people to call and report suspected cases of abuse. Reports of child abuse in Florida before the public awareness campaign were less than twenty per year. In the first year after the campaign, there were 25,000 reports of suspected abuse!

Wife Abuse: Criminalization

Wives were treated differently than children. Since most people assume that adult women are capable of reporting their own victimization, there were no calls for implementing reporting laws for battered women. Yet women still had the problem of being victimized behind closed doors. If the shame and stigma of being a battered wife were not bad enough, many state laws actually stipulated that for a wife to charge her husband with assault and battery, she had to be more severely injured than someone who was assaulted by a stranger. The criminal justice system, beginning with the role and actions of the police, traditionally approached wife abuse from various perspectives— denial, acceptance, lack of awareness, and helplessness. Some police departments used "stitch rules" to respond to cases of domestic assault—a wife who was abused had to require a certain number of surgical sutures before a husband could be arrested for assault and battery (Field and Field, 1973). Prosecutors frequently failed to take the complaints of battered women seriously and sent women home with the advice that they should "kiss and make up."

Many law enforcement officials who tried to assist battered wives complained that the wives themselves handcuffed the criminal justice system. Police frequently point out that women attack and even kill police officers who are called on to intervene in domestic violence. Other police officers point to the numerous instances where women who have been beaten fail to file charges against their husbands or withdraw the charges within a few days of the violent episode. Some prosecutors also point out that women frequently fail to follow through in pressing charges. Some women have actually dropped charges at the trial, and one announced that "husbands are supposed to hit their wives, aren't they?" (Parnas, 1967).

Statements, such as the one that claims that husbands are supposed to hit their wives, create a kind of self-fulfilling prophecy where people and prosecutors expect that all battered women will fail to follow through with legal actions. Consequently, police and prosecutors often advise victims against taking legal action. As a result, police and district attorneys are seen as less than sympathetic to the problem of battered women. Organized womens' groups spent much of the 1970s seeking equal protection for battered women. Class action suits were filed to assure that police and prosecutors paid attention to the problem of battered women. In December 1976, women in New York City filed a class-action suit against the New York Police Department, probation officers, and family court employees for failing to prosecute abusive husbands. The police settled out of court in 1977. In 1974, a class action suit was filed against the Cleveland district attorneys for denying battered women equal protection under the law by not following through in prosecution of abusive husbands. That suit was settled by a consent decree ordering prosecutors to change their practices. In Oakland, the police were accused of illegal conduct because of their pattern and practice of discouraging arrests in cases of domestic violence. (See Response (1979) for complete details on the above legal procedures.) In all these class action suits, the central goal was to eliminate the selective inattention to the problem of battered women and "criminalize" violence against women.

At the beginning of the 1970s few states had laws aimed at reducing spousal violence. Today, most states have enacted legislation on domestic violence. Most of the state laws created new civil and criminal legal remedies for persons abused by family or household members. Some state laws specify the powers and duties of the police and courts in handling domestic violence. Some laws mandate social agencies to provide services to violent families. Finally, a number of states have enacted laws that provide funding for battered wife shelters.

Hidden Violence: Few Legal Remedies

The legal remedies that were applied to child abuse and spousal violence have, in general, not been specifically aimed at the hidden forms of family violence. Adolescent victims of violence are technically covered by child abuse statutes, but as we saw in Chapter 5, adolescents are rarely reported as victims of physical child abuse. Sibling violence is covered only by normal laws pertaining to criminal assault. This too is the case for violence toward parents. The only exception to this pattern is that a handful of states enacted reporting laws aimed at victims of elderly abuse.

INTERVENTION IN FAMILY VIOLENCE: COMPASSION OR CONTROL

Once a case of child or wife abuse has been reported and recognized, the next important step is to intervene. What should be done? As we have noted numerous times in this book, the first emotional reaction to child abuse is to call for stiff and harsh penalties to be meted out against abusive parents. In addition to punishing parents, people frequently advise that the children should be taken away from abusive parents. Similarly, removal of elderly victims of abuse from the homes of their abusers is considered an important first step in treating elder abuse.

Physicians Eli Newberger and Alvin Rosenfeld (1977) have noted two competing philosophies that have been applied to treating child abuse. These philosophies are equally applicable to other forms of family violence treatment.

On the one hand is the compassionate approach to abuse. Human service professionals who treat violence and abuse from this perspective approach it with an abundance of human kindness and a nonpunitive outlook on intervention. The compassionate philosophy views the abusive parents as victims themselves. The cause of the abuse may be seen in social and developmental origins, and not in the abuser. Abusive parents, rather than being seen as cold, cruel monsters, are seen as sad, deprived, and needy human beings. Compassionate intervention involves supporting the abuser and his or her family. Homemaker services, health and child care, and other supports are made available to the family.

On the other hand is the control model. The control model involves aggressive use of intervention to limit, and, if necessary, punish the deviant violent behavior. The control approach places full responsibility for actions with the abuser. Control involves removal of the child from the home, separation of the abused wife from her violent spouse, and full criminal prosecution of the offender.

The compassion model has dangers for the clinician and the family. The compassionate clinician may strive to support a family and may actually raise the risk of further violence by relieving the offender from responsibility. A clinician's concern for alienating abusive parents or abusive partners may compromise the clinician's judgement and result in a victim being left at risk. In addition, should the compassionate approach fail to result in positive change, the human service professional may be left feeling demoralized and burned out.

Human service professionals are reluctant to use the control approach, even when the situation literally screams out for action. Clinicians have been heard to say that they were reluctant to use stern measures because "the family has already suffered enough." Sadly, on some occasions, a control approach may actually raise the risks for abused children and women. On one occasion in the state of Rhode Island, a child was removed from a mother who was neglecting the child. The child was placed in a foster home, only to be beaten to death six months later by the foster father. When women flee battering relationships for shelter, this sometimes enrages the husband to the point of homicide, as happened once to a women in Boston who was attacked and killed by her husband a few blocks from the shelter.

There is no easy solution to the control/compassion dilemma. Rosenfeld and Newberger (1977) call for giving compassion *and* control. Assessment and intervention functions should probably be performed by separate individuals. A control approach might be used in assessment, while compassion is reserved for use once the proper course of treatment is prescribed for the family. In the best of all possible worlds, the choice of intervention would not boil down to a choice between protecting the child or woman by removal versus keeping the family together. The best of all possible worlds would involve appropriate measures of legal control and humane support. The following section reviews the standard and useful forms of treatment that have been developed for dealing with domestic violence.

TREATMENT

As we saw in the previous section, any program or policy designed to treat the problem of violence between family members must be capable of *protecting* the victim(s) while preventing further violence—if possible by strengthening the family. Without both of these components, there is no long-term solution to violence in the home.

Treating Child Abuse

Identification and reporting. The first step in treating child abuse is to identify children in need of services. Consequently, considerable effort has been devoted to improving techniques of identifying and reporting cases of child abuse to the proper human service agencies. Such steps involve a variety of efforts, which are coordinated among numerous public and private agencies. First, as we already mentioned, all fifty states enacted legislation that required reporting suspected cases of child abuse. In order to assure that cases would and could be properly identified, public and private agencies engaged in training programs to educate potential reporters about the signs of abuse. These public education and awareness programs greatly increased the number of child abuse reports that were generated. Because of this, states and localities established child abuse hot lines that were staffed twenty-four hours per day. These hot lines were designed to receive reports. Soon states found that they also required twenty-four hour a day response capabilities.

Child welfare services. It should be obvious from the discussion of the incidence of child abuse in Chapter 3 that if all cases of child abuse and violence toward children were reported to public and private social welfare agencies, and if each reported case was fully investigated and provided services, it would tax the existing social welfare system beyond its present means. In many, if not most states, child welfare or protective service workers are already burdened with case loads which are far too large to allow the workers to service the child and family adequately—and this is when people estimate that only one of three child abuse cases is being reported! Some caseworkers have caseloads of thirty to even fifty families, whereas most professionals in the field of social and human services believe that protective workers should serve no more than twenty families at a time.

The optimal situation for child welfare agencies is to be able to respond to problems of child abuse quickly, effectively, and in a manner that treats the causes of abuse, not just the symptoms. Child welfare systems need to be able to provide immediate crisis intervention when children are at risk. In Florida, only 25 percent of reported cases of child abuse are responded to within the first twenty-four hours (Straus, Gelles, and Steinmetz, 1980). This is too slow to protect many of the victims of child abuse. Ideally, a protective service system ought to be able to respond to all reports of child abuse and neglect and be able to supply emergency resources for the child and family immediately, or at least within twenty-four hours of the report.

The nature of the child welfare response is even more important than how fast a response can be made. Professionals in the field of child protection recommend that child welfare agencies be able to provide emergency homemaker services, a hot line to help parents deal with day-to-day crises, transportation, child care services, counseling or referrals for professional counseling, health care, clothing and shelter, access to self-help groups such as Parents Anonymous, and other resources which ease the burden of child care for parents.

Education for parenting. Studies of child abuse often show that violent and abusive parents do not know how to manage or cope with child rearing. Frequently, abusive parents do not understand the basic stages of child development and have unrealistic expectations of their childrens' abilities. Experience shows that an important treatment and prevention technique is to provide educational services so that parents can learn about child development and appropriate discipline techniques (Jeffrey, 1976; Kempe and Helfer, 1974).

Summary. A complete discussion of treating child abuse would require an entire book. We have only provided an overview of the various problems and options available for treatment. One obvious facet of treating child abuse is that since there are multiple causes of abuse, we require multiple services and interventions. Multiservice and multidiscipline teams have been helpful in treating child abuse. It is important to remember that some treatments will be effective for certain families and fail miserably with other families. Parents Anonymous chapters have an outstanding success rate, but only for those parents who choose to participate. Providing dental or health care services might be sufficient to relieve stress on one household, but not be adequate for another family.

Presently, one major problem in providing adequate treatment is dollars and cents. Most state protective service agencies simply do not have the resources to deal with the number of cases of child abuse and neglect that are being reported. Agencies are trying to add professional staff, but, frequently, these staff are inadequately trained to deal with the complex and emotional problems they confront once on the job. In some states, protective service workers have fewer than forty hours of training! A number of states do not even require that protective service workers hold a professional degree.

The goal of protective service is to best serve the child and family. Optimally, this would involve providing the proper mixture of support services and professional counseling to help the family provide adequate care for its children. When such services are rejected by the family or are ineffective, child welfare professionals face the problem of removing the child from the home and finding a suitable placement for the child. Here we come to another can of worms. Locating an adequate placement is a tremendously difficult and complex task. Abused children frequently require more care and attention than the average child. They may have special physical or emotional needs. This can be extremely taxing on a foster family. Since foster families are frequently at a premium, protective workers sometimes find that they are placing a child in a home that has not been adequately screened or assessed. Sometimes, sadly, this places the child at increased risk.

Ultimately, even the best protective service system is one that can only react to cases of child abuse. Adequately treating child abuse may prevent further abuse in that home, but it can never prevent abuse that has already taken place. We will turn to prevention in the final section of the chapter.

Treating Wife Abuse

Treating wife abuse involves different services and different institutions than those brought to bear to ameliorate the problem of child abuse. Because the victims of wife abuse are adults, conventional wisdom leads one to assume that they are able to take care of themselves and are not helpless victims of violence. There are no mandatory reporting laws for wife abuse. Few agencies even bother to keep records of cases of wife abuse. Police records note wife abuse either as "domestic disturbances" or, rarely, as "assault." Hospitals rarely separate cases of wife assault from other emergency cases. There are some adult protective units in social service agencies, but they typically focus their attention on dependent or vulnerable adults—for instance, the elderly.

The main crisis intervention services that victims of wife abuse can turn to are the police, courts, and battered wife shelters.

The police. The American police officer frequently functions as the neighborhood social worker. In cases of child abuse, police are often called upon to intervene in on-going instances of violence or neglect of children, and their primary function in these instances is to report the abuse or neglect to the proper child welfare authorities. But, in cases of wife abuse, the police not only are the first on the scene of on-going violence, but they also are the agents of social control who command the primary power to protect the victims of wife abuse. The sociologists Sarah Berk and Donileen Loseke (1980) note that "As front-line agents of social control in domestic disturbances, police are the proximate representatives of state policy." The alternative social services that are available to women (such as shelters) most often depend on the police for cooperation—police must inform family violence victims of the availability of these services. The police are a crucial link between the victim of wife abuse and treatment programs available in her community.

Police intervention into cases of domestic violence is danger-ous work. As we noted earlier, as many police officers are killed answering domestic disturbance calls as are killed pursuing armed robbers. Domestic disturbance calls are among the least glamorous and least prestigious work officers engage in. Few officers receive medals or promotions because they are effective in handling domestic violence calls.

Because family violence calls are extremely dangerous *and* the rewards are few, police are rarely motivated to get involved in treatment or prevention. Students of family violence have been quite critical of the traditional police reluctance to intervene and ameliorate family violence (Field and Field, 1973; Dobash and Dobash, 1979).

Berk and Loseke (1980) studied the factors that influenced police officers' decisions of how to intervene in wife assault. Examining data from 262 official police reports concerning domestic disturbances in Santa Barbara, California, Berk and Loseke found four factors that were related to whether or not police decided to arrest a violent husband. If the wife-victim signed an arrest warrant, if both husband and wife were present when the police arrived, if the wife alleged that violence had occurred, and if the husband was drunk when the police arrived, all raised the likelihood that an arrest would be made. However, if the wife made the original call to the police, this actually reduced the chances that the husband would be arrested. Thus, the traditional complaint that police do not effectively intervene because they, as an occupational group, support the right of husbands to hit their wives and the complaint that the police are reluctant to get involved in "family matters" does not seem to hold under analysis. The data suggest that situational factors, not occupational attitudes, affect police decision making.

How important is it that the police actually arrest a wife abuser? Certainly there are other options available to police officers when they enter a violent home. Police officers could separate the combatants and remove the husband from the home so that he could "cool down." A number of communities have invested in training programs for their police officers to teach them how to counsel the violent parties. Some communities have created domestic violence units that team up police officers with social workers. Given these options, why be concerned with arrest? A recent study, conducted by the Police Foundation, points to the importance of arrest. The Police Foundation, in cooperation with the police chief of the city of Minneapolis, Minnesota, set up an experiment. Realizing that police officers use situational factors to determine who to arrest, the experimenters chose to remove these situational factors from the decision and then to assess what effect arrest would have. Thus, police officers were randomly assigned, before they went on a call, to one of three conditions: arrest the offender; order the offender out of the house for up to eight hours; try to mediate the dispute. Situational factors could not influence the decision; the police knew when they left on the call that no matter what they found, they would either arrest or not arrest. The purpose of the experiment was to follow up the cases of domestic violence and see what affect the arrest had. The results were informative. Arrested husbands were less likely to hit their wives again. Clearly, the police are not only on the front line, but they have an intervention alternative (arrest) that, at least for this one study, is demonstrated to be quite effective in reducing the risk of future violence.

The courts. The second line of defense for an adult victim of domestic violence is the court system. Court imposed intervention includes the issuance of protective orders or restraining orders to keep violent husbands out of the home and away from their wives and children. Peace bonds are frequently imposed along with these orders to add the deterrent effect of lost money should the order be violated. Prosecution for less than lethal family violence is still problematic, and the courts still retain vestiges of viewing domestic violence as "family matters."

Shelters. Perhaps the most important development in the last twenty years in treating wife abuse has been the grassroots development of battered wife shelters or safe houses. One of the first shelters designed to protect victims of family violence was created almost by accident. As we mentioned in Chapter 2, in 1971, a group of women in Chiswick, England, met to discuss rising food prices. But prices were not their biggest complaint—loneliness was. Out of these first meetings a Women's Aid project was established by Erin Pizzey. Soon a house was set up as Chiswick Women's Aid. The house became a center for women with personal problems. Before long, the house filled up with women with a common problem—wife abuse. Within three years, Women's Aid of Chiswick became the model for women's shelters around the world.

In 1976, there were probably no more than five or six shelters in the United States. By 1984, there may well be over 500, and the list grows every day. Some shelters are established by feminist groups. Other shelters are set up by social service agencies. Some shelters actually are the result of class projects organized by students enrolled in family violence courses at colleges and universities. Nearly every shelter established was established through volunteer effort and donations. Few, if any shelters, were blessed with government or foundation funding. Budgets are typically small, furniture donated, and staff time volunteered.

The concept of a shelter, safe house, or refuge, is quite simple and solves a basic problem for the battered wife—it provides her and her children a place to go. Because wife abuse and family violence often happen on weekends, at nights, or in the dead of winter, there is frequently no place a victim can turn for help (except the police). Battered wives in bathrobes have spent hours walking the freezing streets. Shelters provide protection for the victim or potential victim of a violent assault. In addition, shelters often make referrals for legal and marriage counseling, help women find jobs, and above all, help restore the sense of self-esteem that women have typically lost after years of psychological and physical battering.

Shelters have various capabilities, abilities, and rules. Some can hold thirty women, some can hold but a few. Most women seem to stay for a week or two before they leave. Although there is no valid documentation, it appears that about one-third of the women who come to shelters do not return to their violent mate. The other two-thirds do return, some to more violence, others to try and change their marital arrangement and eliminate violence as a way of life. To date, there have been few systematic studies of the impact and effect of shelters. They are, however, one of the few oases in the storm of violence that are available for battered women.

Men's groups. Since 1980, there have been a number of men's counseling groups established with the purpose of counseling violent men. Emerge in Boston, Brother to Brother in Providence, Rhode Island, and a number of other organizations around the country have been organized by men with the goal of counseling violent men. To date, the number of such programs is small, and the number of men each group counsels is also quite modest. It is however, a constructive attempt to treat family violence and change social attitudes about the appropriateness of hitting family members.

Other Forms of Family Violence

As we noted in Chapter 5, violent relations other than parent to child and husband to wife have long been hidden from public attention. Thus, with only rare exceptions, there are few treatment programs for sibling violence, violence toward parents, and violence toward the elderly. If these forms of violence are recognized and treated at all, they typically are dealt with through traditional individual and family counseling.

Mandatory elder abuse reporting laws have been passed in some states. The results have been mixed. Adult protective service workers have found that elderly victims of violence have been extremely reluctant to leave violent and abusive homes. The fear of being institutionalized seems to outweigh the pain and suffering some elderly experience. Thus, adult protective service workers often invest countless hours investigating reports of elder abuse, only to find the victim reluctant to accept any form of treatment.

To our knowledge, there are no self-help groups for victims of parent abuse. Most parents still seem to be suffering in silence and shame. Violent siblings, unless they maim or kill a brother or sister, are not even recognized as violent, let alone attended to with treatment or intervention.

One of the roadblocks to effective treatment for the hidden forms of family violence is the fact that child abuse and wife abuse were recognized and treated by completely separate institutions and systems. There is little, if any, overlap in the treatment programs aimed at either child or wife abuse. There is little recognition of the problem of *family violence*. Each group identifies their own problems, develops their own treatment, secures their own funds, and, in an era of scarce money for social services, jealously guards their own turf. One of the notable gaps in the entire treatment program is a recognition of the problem of family violence and the development of treatment modalities for the whole family and the entire range of the problem.

PREVENTION

Treatment is necessary to protect the lives and welfare of the victims or potential victims of family violence. But even the implementation of effective and efficient treatment programs will not break the cycle of cultural norms and values that contribute to the violent nature of the family. Nor do treatment programs alone alter the characteristics of society and the family that increase the risk that certain families will be violent and abusive.

The cental goal of programs and policies aimed at family violence is to prevent violence. The findings presented in this book clearly point to the fact that some fundamental changes in values and beliefs will have to occur before we see a real decrease in the level of violence in the family. Looking toward the future, there are a number of policy steps that could help prevent intimate violence.

1. *Eliminate the norms that legitimize and glorify violence in the society and the family.* The elimination of spanking as a child rearing technique, gun control to get deadly weapons out of the home, elimination of corporal punishment in school and the death penalty, and an elimination of media violence which glorifies and legitimizes violence are all necessary steps. In short, we need to cancel the hitting license in society.

2. *Reduce violence-provoking stress created by society.* Reducing poverty, inequality, unemployment and providing for adequate housing, feeding, medical and dental care, and educational opportunities are steps which could reduce stress in families.

3. *Integrate families into a network of kin and community.* Reducing social isolation would be a significant step that would help reduce stress and increase the abilities of families to manage stress.

4. *Change the sexist character of society.* Sexual inequality, perhaps more than economic inequality, makes violence possible in homes. The elimination of men's work and women's work would be a major step toward equality in and out of the home.

5. *Break the cycle of violence in the family.* This step repeats the message of step 1—violence can not be prevented as long as we are taught that it is appropriate to hit the people we love. Physical punishment of children is perhaps the most effective means of teaching violence, and eliminating it would be an important step in violence prevention.

Such steps require long-term changes in the fabric of society. These proposals call for such fundamental change in families and family life that many people resist them and argue that they could not work or would ruin the family. The alternative, of course, is that not making such changes continues the harmful and deadly tradition of family violence.

DISCUSSION QUESTIONS

1. How do police expectations about battered women being prone to drop charges against their abusive husbands create a self-fulfilling prophecy and deny women their proper legal rights of protection?

2. What legal remedies could be enacted to deal with the problems of hidden family violence—elderly abuse, sibling violence, parent abuse, abuse of adolescents?

3. Give an example of how compassion and control could be used to intervene in cases of child abuse, wife abuse, abuse of the elderly.

SUGGESTED ASSIGNMENTS

1. Create a resource guide that lists the community services (names, addresses, and telephone numbers) of agencies and organizations that deal with various aspects of family violence.

References

ADELSON, L. (1972) "The battering child." Journal of the American Medical Association 222 (October): 159-161.

ALFARO, J. (1977) "Report on the relationship between child abuse and neglect and later socially deviant behavior." Presented at a symposium, Exploring the Relationship Between Child Abuse and Delinquency, Seattle, University of Washington, July 21-22.

American Humane Association (1980) National Analysis of Official Child Neglect and Abuse Reporting. Englewood, CO: American Humane Association.

ARIES, P. (1962) Centuries of Childhood. New York: Knopf.

BALL, M. (1977) "Issues of violence in family casework." Social Casework 58 (January): 3-12.

BARD, M. (1969) "Family intervention police teams as a community mental health resource." Journal of Criminal Law, Criminology, and Police Science 60 (2): 247-250.

————and J. ZACKER (1971) "The prevention of family violence: Dilemmas of community intervention." Journal of Marriage and the Family 33 (4): 677-682.

BENDER, L. (1959) "Children and adolescents who have killed." American Journal of Psychiatry 116 (December): 510-513.

BERK, S. and D. LOSEKE (1980) "'Handling' family violence: The situated determinants of police arrest in domestic disturbances." Law and Society Review 15 (2): 317-346.

BERK, R., S. F. BERK, D. R. LOSEKE, and D. RAUMA (1983) "Mutual combat and other family violence myths," pp. 197-212 in D. Finkelhor et al. (eds.) The Dark Side of Families: Current Family Violence Research. Beverly Hills, CA: Sage.

BLAU, P. M. (1964) Exchange and Power in Social Life. New York: Wiley.

BLOCK, M. and J. SINNOTT (1979) "Battered elder syndrome: An exploratory study." (unpublished, University of Maryland)

BLUMBERG, M. (1964) "When parents hit out." Twentieth Century 173 (Winter): 39-44.

BOUDOURIS, J. (1971) "Homicide and the family." Journal of Marriage and the Family 33 (November): 667-682.

BOWKER, L. H. (1983) Beating Wife-Beating. Lexington, MA: Lexington Books.

BREKKE, J. and D. SAUNDERS (1982) "Research on woman abuse: A review of findings, needs, and issues." (unpublished)

BRILEY, M. (1979) "Battered parents." Dynamic Years 14 (January/February): 24-27.

BRONFENBRENNER, U. (1958) "Socialization and social class throughout time and space," pp. 400-425 in E. Maccoby et al. (eds.) Readings in Social Psychology. New York: Holt.

BURGDORF, K. (1980) Recognition and Reporting of Child Maltreatment. Rockville, MD: Westat.

BUTTON, A. (1973) "Some antecedents of felonious and delinquent behavior." Journal of Clinical Child Psychology 2 (Fall): 35-38.

BYRD, D. E. (1979) "Intersexual assault: A review of empirical findings." Presented at the annual meetings of the Eastern Sociological Society, New York.

CAFFEY, J. (1946) "Multiple fractures in the long bones of infants suffering from chronic subdural hematoma." American Journal of Roentgenology, Radium Therapy, and Nuclear Medicine 58: 163-173.

CALVERT, R. (1974) "Criminal and civil liability in husband-wife assaults" pp. 88-90 in S. Steinmetz and M. Straus (eds.) Violence in the Family. New York: Harper & Row.

CARR, A. (1977) Some Preliminary Findings on the Association Between Child Maltreatment and Juvenile Misconduct in Eight New York Counties. Report to the

Administration for Children, Youth and Families, National Center on Child Abuse and Neglect (October 20).

CATE, R. M., J. M. HENTON, F. S. CHRISTOPHER, and S. LLOYD (1982) "Premarital abuse: A social psychological perspective." Journal of Family Issues 3 (March): 79-90.

CORNELL, C. P. and R. J. GELLES (1982) "Adolescent to parent violence." Urban Social Change Review 15 (Winter): 8-14.

CURTIS, L. (1974) Criminal Violence: National Patterns and Behavior. Lexington, MA: Lexington Books.

D'AGOSTINO, S. (1983) "Finally, judgement." Worcester Magazine (August 17): 11-13.

DAVIDSON, T. (1978) Conjugal Crime: Understanding and Changing the Wifebeating Pattern. New York: Hawthorn Books.

DeMAUSE, L. [ed.] (1974) The History of Childhood. New York: Psychohistory Press.

DOBASH, R. E. and R. DOBASH (1979) Violence Against Wives. New York: Free Press.

EDGERTON, R. B. (1981) "Forward to child abuse and neglect: Cross-cultural perspectives," pp. vii-viii in J. Korbin (ed.) Child Abuse and Neglect: Cross-Cultural Perspectives. Berkeley: University of California Press.

ELMER, E. (1967) Children in Jeopardy: A Study of Abused Minors and Their Families. Pittsburgh: University of Pittsburgh Press.

ERLANGER, H. (1974) "Social class and corporal punishment in childrearing: A reassessment." American Sociological Review 39 (February): 68-85.

ETZIONI, A. (1971) "Violence," pp. 709-741 in R. K. Merton and R. Nisbet (eds.) Contemporary Social Problems. New York: Harcourt Brace Jovanovich.

FAGAN, J. A., D. K. STEWART, and K. W. STEWART (1983) "Situational correlates of domestic and extra-domestic violence," pp. 49-67 in D. Finkelhor et al. (eds.) The Dark Side of Families: Current Family Violence Research. Beverly Hills, CA: Sage.

FERGUSSON, D. M., J. FLEMING, and D. O'NEIL (1972) Child Abuse in New Zealand. Wellington, New Zealand: Research Division, Department of Social Work.

FERREIRA, A. (1963) "Family myth and homeostasis." Archives of General Psychiatry 9 (5): 451-463.

FIELD, M. and H. FIELD (1973) "Marital violence and the criminal process: Neither justice nor peace." Social Service Review 47 (2): 221-240.

FINKELHOR, D. (1983) "Common features of family abuse," pp. 17-28 in D. Finkelhor et al. (eds.) The Dark Side of Families: Current Family Violence Research. Beverly Hills CA: Sage.

———and K. YLLO (1982) "Forced sex in marriage: A preliminary report." Crime and Delinquency 28: 459-478.

FONTANA, V. (1973) Somewhere a Child is Crying: Maltreatment— Causes and Prevention. New York: Macmillan.

FRIEDRICH, W. N. and J. A. BORISKIN (1976) "The role of the child in abuse: A review of literature." American Journal of Orthopsychiatry 46 (4): 580-590.

GALDSTON, R. (1965) "Observations of children who have been physically abused by their parents." American Journal of Psychiatry 122 (4): 440-443.

———(1975) "Preventing abuse of little children: The parent's center project for the study and prevention of child abuse." American Journal or Orthopsychiatry 45 (April): 372-381.

GARBARINO, J. (1977) "The human ecology of child maltreatment." Journal of Marriage and the Family 39 (4): 721-735.

————and G. GILLIAM (1980) Understanding Abusive Families. Lexington, MA: D. C. Heath.

GAYFORD, J. J. (1975) "Wife battering: A preliminary survey of 100 cases." British Medical Journal 1 (January): 194-197.

GELLES, R. (1973) "Child abuse as psychopathology: A sociological critique and reformulation." American Journal of Orthopsychiatry 43 (July): 611-621.

————(1974) The Violent Home. Beverly Hills, CA: Sage.

————(1975) "The social construction of child abuse." American Journal of Orthopsychiatry 45 (April): 363-371.

————(1976) "Abused wives: Why do they stay?" Journal of Mariage and the Family 38 (November): 659-668.

————(1977) "Power, sex, and violence: The case of marital rape." Family Coordinator 26 (October): 339-347.

————and C. P. CORNELL [eds.] (1983) International Perspectives on Family Violence. Lexington, MA: Lexington Books.

GELLES, R. and E. HARGREAVES (1981) "Maternal employment and violence towards children." Journal of Family Issues 2 (December): 509-530.

GELLES, R. and M. STRAUS (1979) "Determinants of violence in the family: Toward a theoretical integration," pp. 549-581 in W. R. Burr et al. (eds.) Contemporary Theories About the Family (vol. 1). New York: Free Press.

GIL, D. (1970) Violence Against Children: Physical Child Abuse in the United States. Cambridge, MA: Harvard University Press.

GILLEN, J. (1946) The Wisconsin Prisoner: Studies in Crimogenesis. Madison: University of Wisconsin Press.

GIOVANNONI, J. M. and R. M. BECERRA (1979) Defining Child Abuse. New York: Free Press.

GOODE, W. (1971) "Force and violence in the family." Journal of Marriage and the Family 33 (November): 624-636.

GUTTMACHER, M. (1960) The Mind of the Murderer. New York: Farrar, Straus, and Cudahy.

HARBIN, H. and D. MADDEN (1979) "Battered parents: A new syndrome." American Journal of Psychiatry 136 (October): 1288-1291.

HENTON, J., R. CATE, J. KOVAL, S. LLOYD, and S. CHRISTOPHER (1983) "Romance and violence in dating relationships." Journal of Family Issues 4 (September): 467-482.

HILBERMAN, E. and K. MUNSON. (1977) "Sixty battered women." Victimology 2 (3 & 4): 460-470.

HOMANS, G. C. (1967) "Fundamental social processes," pp. 27-78 in N. Smelser (ed.) Sociology. New York: Wiley.

HORNUNG, C., B. McCULLOUGH, and T. SUGIMOTO (1981) "Status relationships in marriage: Risk factors in spouse abuse." Journal of Marriage and the Family 43 (August): 679-692.

JASON, J., M. CARPENTER, and C. TYLER, Jr. (1983a) "Underrecording of infant homicide in the United States." American Journal of Public Health 73: 195-197.

JASON, J., J. GILLILAND, and C. TYLER, Jr. (1983b) "Homicide as a cause of pediatric mortality in the United States." Pediatrics 72 (2): 191-197.

JEFFREY, M. (1976) "Practical ways to change parent-child interaction in families of children at risk," pp. 209-224 in R. Helfer and C. H. Kempe (eds.) Child Abuse and Neglect: The Family and the Community. Cambridge, MA: Ballinger.

JOHNSON, B. and H. MORSE. (1968) The Battered Child: A Study of Children With Inflicted Injuries. Denver, CO: Denver Department of Welfare.

JOHNSON, C. (1974) Child Abuse in the Southeast: An Analysis of 1172 Reported Cases. Athens, GA: Welfare Research.

JONES, A. (1980) Women Who Kill. New York: Holt, Rinehart, & Winston.

KAMERMAN, S. (1975) "Eight countries: Cross national perspectives on child abuse and neglect." Children Today 4 (3): 34-37.

KEMPE, C. H. (1973) "A practical approach to the protection of the abused child: Rehabilitating the abusing parent." Pediatrics 51 (11): 804-809.

———and R. HELFER (1974) Helping the Battered Child and His Family. Philadelphia: Lippincott.

KEMPE, C. H., F. N. SILVERMAN, B. F. STEELE, W. DROEGEMUELLER, and H. K. SILVER (1962) "The battered child syndrome." Journal of the American Medical Association 181: 107-112.

KOCH, L. and J. KOCH (1980) "Parent abuse—A new plague." Washington Post (January 27): PA14-15.

KOHN, M. (1977) Class and Conformity: A Study of Values. Chicago: University of Chicago Press.

KORBIN, J. [ed.] (1981) Child Abuse and Neglect: Cross-Cultural Perspectives. Berkeley: University of California Press.

LANER, M., J. THAMPSON, and R. GRAHAM (1981) "Abuse and aggression in courting couples." Presented at the annual meetings of the Western Social Science Association, San Diego.

LASLETT, B. (1978) "The family as a public and private institution: A historical perspective." Journal of Marriage and the Family 35 (August): 480-492.

———(1973) "Family membership, past and present." Social Problems 25 (5): 476-490.

LAU, E. E. and J. I. KOSBERG (1979) "Abuse of the elderly by informal care providers." Aging 299 (Summer): 10-15.

LAUER, B. (1974) "Battered child syndrome: Review of 130 patients with controls." Pediatrics 54 (1): 67-70.

Le MASTERS, E. (1957) "Parenthood as crisis." Marriage and Family Living 19 (November): 352-355.

Legal Research and Services for the Elderly (1979) Elder abuse in Massachusetts: A survey of professionals and paraprofessionals. (unpublished)

LEVINGER, G. (1966) "Sources of marital dissatisfaction among applicants for divorce." American Journal of Orthopsychiatry 26 (October): 803-897.

LEVINSON, D. (1981) "Physical punishment of children and wifebeating in cross-cultural perspective." Child Abuse and Neglect 5 (4): 193-196.

LIGHT, R. J. (1974) "Abused and neglected children in America: A study of alternative policies." Harvard Educational Review 43 (November): 556-598.

LONDON, J. (1978) "Images of violence against women." Victimology 2 (3/4): 510-524.

LYMAN, S. and M. SCOTT (1970) A Sociology of the Absurd. New York: Appleton-Century-Crofts.

MacANDREW, C. and R. B. EDGERTON (1969) Drunken Comportment: A Social Explanation. Chicago: Aldine.

MAKEPIECE, J. (1981) "Courtship violence among college students." Family Relations 30 (January): 97-102.

———(1983) "Life events-stress and courtship violence." Family Relations 32 (1): 101-109.

MARTIN, H. P., P. BEEZLEY, E. G. CONWAY, and C. H. KEMPE (1974) "The devel-
    opment of abused children," in I. Schulman (ed.) Advances in Pediatrics (vol. 21).
    Chicago: Yearbook Medical Publishers.
MARTIN, M. J. and J. WALTERS (1982) "Familial correlates of selected types of child
    abuse and neglect." Journal of Marriage and the Family 44 (2): 267-276.
MAURER, A. (1976) "Physical punishment of chilren." Presented at the California State
    Psychological Convention, Anaheim.
MERTON, R. K. (1945) "Sociological theory." American Journal of Sociology 50 (May):
    462-473.
MILLS, C. W. (1940) "Situated actions and vocabularies of motive." American Sociolog-
    ical Review 5 (October): 904-913.
MULLIGAN, M. (1977) "An investigation of factors associated with violent modes of
    conflict resolution in the family." M.A. thesis, University of Rhode Island.
NAGI, R. (1975) "Child abuse and neglect programs: A national overview." Children
    Today 4 (May-June): 13-17.
NEWBERGER, E. et al. (1977) "Pediatric social illness: Toward an etiologic classifica-
    tion." Pediatrics 60 (August): 178-185.
NYE, F. I. (1979) "Choice, exchange, and the family," pp. 1-41 in W. R. Burr et al. (eds.)
    Contemporary Theories About the Family (vol. 2). New York: Free Press.
O'BRIEN, J. (1971) "Violence in divorce prone families." Journal of Marriage and the
    Family 33 (November): 692-698.
OWENS, D. and M. A. STRAUS (1975) "Childhood violence and adult approval of
    violence." Aggressive Behavior 1 (2): 193-211.
PAGELOW, M. (1981) Woman-Battering: Victims and Their Experiences. Beverly Hills,
    CA: Sage.
PARKE, R. D. and C. W. COLLMER (1975) "Child abuse: an interdisciplinary analysis,"
    pp. 1-102 in M. Hetherington (ed.) Review of Child Development Research, (vol 5).
    Chicago: University of Chicago Press.
PARNAS, R. (1967) "The police response to domestic disturbance." Wisconsin Law
    Review 914 (Fall): 914-960.
PITTMAN, D. and W. HANDY (1964) "Patterns in criminal aggravated assault." Journal
    of Criminal Law, Criminology, and Police Science 55 (4): 462-470.
PIZZEY, E. (1974) Scream Quietly or the Neighbors Will Hear. Harmondsworth, Great
    Britain: Penguin.
PLECK, E., J. PLECK, M. GROSSMAN, and P. BART (1978) "The battered data
    syndrome: A comment on Steinmetz's article." Victimology 2 (3/4): 680-683.
POKORNY, A. (1965) "Human violence: A comparison of homicide, aggravated assault,
    suicide, and attempted suicide." Journal of Criminal Law, Criminology, and Police
    Science 56 (December): 488-497.
PRESCOTT, S. and C. LETKO (1977) "Battered women: A social psychological perspec-
    tive," pp. 72-96 in M. Roy (ed.) Battered Women: A Psychosociological Study of
    Domestic Violence. New York: Van Nostrand Reinhold.
RADBILL, S. (1980) "A history of child abuse and infanticide," pp. 3-20 in R. Helfer and C.
    Kempe (eds.) The Battered Child (3rd ed.). Chicago: University of Chicago Press.
RATHBONE-McCUAN, E. (1980) "Elderly victims of family violence and neglect." Social
    Casework 61 (May): 296-304.
Response (1979) "Battered women press police for equal protection." Response 2 (6): 3.
———(1983) "State legislation on domestic violence." Response 6 (5): 1-5.

ROBIN, M. (1983) "Historical introduction: Sheltering arms: The roots of child protection," pp. 1-41 in E. H. Newberger (ed.) Child Abuse. Boston: Little, Brown.

ROSENFELD, A. and E. H. NEWBERGER (1977) "Compassion vs. control: Conceptual and practical pitfalls in the broadened definition of child abuse." Journal of the American Medical Association 237: 2086-2088.

ROSSI, A. (1968) "Transition to parenthood." Journal of Marriage and the Family 30 (February): 26-39.

ROUNSAVILLE, B. J. (1978) "Theories of marital violence: Evidence from a study of battered women." Victimology 3 (1 and 2): 11-31.

ROY, M. (1977) Battered Women: A Psychosocial Study of Domestic Violence. New York: Van Nostrand Reinhold.

RUSSELL, D. (1980) "The prevalence and impact of marital rape in San Francisco." Presented at the annual meeting of the American Sociological Association, New York.

SARGENT, D. (1962) "Children who kill—A family conspiracy." Social Work 7 (January): 35-42.

SCHMITT, B. and C. H. KEMPE (1975) "Neglect and abuse of children," in V. Vaughan and R. McKay (eds.) Nelson Textbook of Pediatrics. Philadelphia: W. B. Saunders.

SCHULTZ, L. G. (1960) "The wife assaulter." Journal of Social Therapy 6 (2): 103-111.

SHAINESS, N. (1977) "Psychological aspects of wife battering," pp. 111-119 in M. Roy (ed.) Battered Women: A Psychosocial Study of Domestic Violence. New York: Van Nostrand Reinhold.

SIMMEL, G. (1950) The sociology of Georg Simmel (K. Wolf, ed.). New York: Free Press.

SMITH, S. (1965) "The adolescent murderer." Archives of General Psychiatry 13 (October): 310-319.

———(1975) The Battered Child Syndrome. London: Buttersworth.

———R. HANSEN, and S. NOBLE (1973) "Parents of battered babies: A controlled study." British Medical Journal 5 (5889): 388-391.

SMITH, S., L. HONIGSBERGER, and C. SMITH (1973) "E.E.G. and personality factors in baby batterers," British Medical Journal 2 (July): 20-22.

SNELL, J. E., R. J. ROSENWALD, and ROBEY (1964) "The wifebeater's wife: A study of family interaction." Archives of General Psychiatry 11 (August): 107-113.

STARK, R. and J. McEVOY (1970) "Middle class violence." Psychology Today 4 (November): 52-65.

STEELE, B. F. (1978) "The child abuser," pp. 285-300 in I. Kutash et al. (eds.) Violence: Perspectives on Murder and Aggression. San Francisco: Jossey-Bass.

———and C. POLLOCK (1968) "A psychiatric study of parents who abuse infants and small children," pp. 103-147 in R. Helfer and C. Kempe (eds.) The Battered Child. Chicago: University of Chicago Press.

———(1974) "A psychiatric study of parents who abuse infants and small children," pp. 89-134 in R. Helfer and C. Kempe (eds.) The Battered Child (2nd ed.). Chicago: University of Chicago Press.

STEINMETZ, S. K. (1971) "Occupation and physical punishment: A response to Straus." Journal of Marriage and the Family 33 (November): 664-666.

———(1977) The Cycle of Violence: Assertive, Aggressive, and Abusive Family Interaction. New York: Praeger Publishers.

———(1978a) "The battered husband syndrome." Victimology 2 (3/4): 499-509.

———(1978b) "Violence between family members." Marriage and Family Review 1 (3): 1-16.

———(1978c) "Battered parents." Society 15 (5): 54-55.

———and M. STRAUS (1974) Violence in the Family. New York: Harper & Row.

STRAUS, M. (1971) "Some social antecedents of physical punishment: A linkage theory interpretation." Journal of Marriage and the Family 33 (November): 658-663.

———(1980) "A sociological perspective on the causes of family violence," pp. 7-31 in M. R. Green (ed.) Violence and the Family. Boulder, CO: Westview Press.

———R. GELLES, and S. K. STEINMETZ (1976) "Violence in the family: An assessment of knowledge and research needs." Presented to the American Association for the Advancement of Science, Boston.

———(1980) Behind Closed Doors: Violence in the American Family. Garden City, NY: Anchor Press.

STRAUS, M. and G. HOTALING (1979) The Social Causes of Husband-Wife Violence. Minneapolis: University of Minnesota Press.

TOBY, J. (1966) "Violence and the masculine ideal: Some qualitative data." Annals of the American Academy of Political and Social Science 364: 20-27.

TRUNINGER, E. (1971) "Marital violence: The legal solutions." Hastings Law Review 23 (November): 259-276.

TURBETT, J. P. and R. O'TOOLE (1980) "Physician's recognition of child abuse." Presented at the annual meeting of the American Sociological Association, New York.

U.S. Bureau of the Census (1978) Statistical Abstracts of the United States. Washington, DC: U.S. Department of Commerce.

U.S. Department of Justice (1980) Intimate Victims: A Study of Violence Among Friends and Relatives. Washington, DC: Government Printing Office

———(1981) Uniform Crime Reports, 1980. Washington, DC: Government Printing Office.

U.S. Senate (1973) Hearing Before the Subcommittee on Children and Youth of the Committee on Labor and Public Welfare. United States Senate, 93rd Congress, first session, on S.1191 Child Abuse Prevention Act. Washington, DC: Government Printing Office.

VESTERDAL, J. (1977) "Handling of child abuse in Denmark," Child Abuse and Neglect 1 (1): 193-198.

WALKER, L. (1979) The Battered Woman. New York: Harper & Row.

WARREN, C. (1978) "Battered parents: Adolescent violence and the family." Presented to the Pacific Sociological Association.

WASSERMAN, S. (1967) "The abused parent of the abused child." Children 14 (September-October): 175-179.

WEITZMAN J. and K. DREEN (1982) "Wife-beating: A view of the marital dyad." Social Casework 63 (5):

WERTHAM, F. (1972) "Battered children and baffled parents." Bulletin of the New York Academy of Medicine 48: 888-898.

WOLFGANG, M. (1958) Patterns in Criminal Homicide. New York: John Wiley.

WRIGHT, L. (1971) "The 'sick but slick' syndrome as a personality component for parents of battered children." Journal of Clinical Psychology 32 (1): 41-45.

YOUNG, L. (1964) Wednesday's Child: A Study of Child Neglect and Abuse. New York: McGraw-Hill.

ZALBA, S. (1971) "Battered children." Transaction 8 (July-August): 58-61.

Author Index

Subject Index

Abortion, 27, 34
Abusive violence, 23-24, 49-50
Abuser
    child abuser, 51, 54-56, 122
    power issues, 71, 75
    social class of, 56, 73
    spouse abuser, 18, 71, 72-73, 122
    treatment, 142
    working mothers, 56
Adolescent violence
    characteristics of abused, 94-95
    frequency of, 93-94
    normative attitudes toward, 91
    parental expectations, 92
    prevention, 132
    size and strength of abuser, 92-93
Age
    of victim, 50, 54, 89-90, 94-95, 104, 125
    of abuser, 56, 73, 99, 104
Alcohol, 18-19, 55, 72, 114, 123
American Humane Association, 47, 53
Appropriate victims of family violence, 30-33, 65
Assault, 23

"Battered Child Syndrome," 20
Biblical accounts
    of child abuse, 28
    of spouse abuse, 30-31
Blaming the victim, 18, 66, 67, 84, 91, 92, 97, 102

Canada, rates of family violence, 32
Child abuse, 14, 27-30, 42, 45-52
    and value of children, 35
    child factors as contributing to, 118
    cross-cultural studies of, 33
    definition of, 20-24, 48
    diagnosis of, 17, 29, 42

    frequency of, 43, 45
    historical legacy of, 27-30
    legislation, 29-30, 32
    profile of violent home, 108-109
    reporting programs, 52, 129-130
    treatment programs for, 30, 134-135
Child Abuse Prevention Act, 30
Child factors as associated with child abuse, 54,
    118, 123
Child welfare services, 135-136
China and family violence, 34, 35
Compassion model, 128, 132-134
Conflict tactics scale, 48, 69
Consequences of child abuse, 59-60
Contemporary attitudes of family violence, 36-38
Contraceptives, 34
Control model, 133-134
Courts' involvement in domestic violence, 140
Courtship violence
    frequency, 65-66
    romantic illusions, 66
Criminal assault, 67-68
Criminal justice system, 26, 29, 32, 42, 68, 128,
    130, 140-141
Criminalization of spouse abuse, 130-132
Cross-cultural studies of violence
    alcohol as related to, 19
    attitudes toward women and children, 35-36
    causes of, 33-34
    definitions of abuses, 32
    frequency of, 33
Culpability as related to wife abuse, 18, 20, 67
Cultural attitudes toward family violence, 22, 35,
    37, 38, 115-116, 117, 125, 144
"Cycle of Violence" theory, 17-18, 38, 42, 57-58,
    74, 100, 105, 128, 144
    in China, 35

157

About the Authors

Richard J. Gelles is Dean of the College of Arts and Sciences, professor of sociology and anthropology at the University of Rhode Island, and lecturer on pediatrics at the Harvard Medical School. He directs the Family Violence Research Program at the University of Rhode Island and has published extensively on the topics of child abuse, wife abuse, and family violence. He is the author of *The Violent Home* (1974) and *Family Violence* (1979), coauthor of *Behind Closed Doors: Violence in the American Family* (1980), and coeditor of *The Dark Side of Families: Current Family Violence Research* (1983) and *International Perspectives on Family Violence* (1983).

Claire Pedrick Cornell is currently an education specialist with the Rhode Island Department of Higher Education. She was formerly a special instructor of socioloy at the University of Rhode Island and a research analyst with the Family Violence Research Program at the University of Rhode Island. Her research interests include child abuse, spouse abuse, adolescent violence, and abuse of the elderly. She is coeditor of *International Perspectives on Family Violence* (1983).